Ninja Foodi XL Pro Air Fry Toaster Oven Cookbook 1000

1000-Day Tasty, Healthy, and Affordable Air Fry Oven Recipes for Everyone to Air Fry, Roast, Bake, Broil, Toast, Bagel, Dehydrate and More

By Kenzi Lewis

© Copyright 2020-All rights reserved.

In no way is it legal to reproduce, duplicate, or transmit any part of this document by either electronic means or in printed format. Recording of this publication is strictly prohibited, and any storage of this material is not allowed unless with written permission from the publisher. All rights reserved.

The information provided herein is stated to be truthful and consistent, in that any liability, regarding inattention or otherwise, by any usage or abuse of any policies, processes, or directions contained within is the solitary and complete responsibility of the recipient reader. Under no circumstances will any legal liability or blame be held against the publisher for any reparation, damages, or monetary loss due to the information herein, either directly or indirectly.

Respective authors own all copyrights not held by the publisher.

Legal Notice:

This book is copyright protected. This is only for personal use. You cannot amend, distribute, sell, use, quote or paraphrase any part or the content within this book without the consent of the author or copyright owner. Legal action will be pursued if this is breached.

Disclaimer Notice:

Please note the information contained within this document is for educational and entertainment purposes only. Every attempt has been made to provide accurate, up to date and reliable, complete information. No warranties of any kind are expressed or implied. Readers acknowledge that the author is not engaging in the rendering of legal, financial, medical or professional advice.

By reading this document, the reader agrees that under no circumstances are we responsible for any losses, direct or indirect, which are incurred as a result of the use of information contained within this document, including, but not limited to, —errors, omissions, or inaccuracies.

Table of content

Description 1
Introduction 2
Chapter 1: Ninja Foodi 10-in-1 XL Pro Air fry Toaster Oven 101 3
    What is the Ninja Foodi 10-in-1 XL Pro Air fry Toaster Oven? ... 3
    Functions of the Ninja Foodi 10-in-1 XL Pro Air fry Toaster Oven 4
Chapter 2: Tips for Usage, Maintenance, and Cleaning 6
Chapter 3: Frequently Asked Questions 7
Chapter 4: Brunch Recipes 8
    Apple Baby Pancake 8
    Bacon and Cheese Frittata 9
    Fluffy Frittata 10
    Crispy Cheesy Hash Brown Casserole 11
    Greek Feta Baked Omelet 12
    Baked Eggs in Brioche 13
    Parmesan Baked Eggs 14
    Sweet-and-Spicy Bacon 15
    Crispy French Fries 16
    Cherry Almond Breakfast Scones 17
Chapter 5: Beef, Pork, and Lamb Recipes 18
    Dry-Rubbed Flat Iron Steak 18
    Steak Seared in Browned Butter 19
    Comforting Red Wine Steak 20
    Flank Steak Fajitas 21
    Peppercorn Pork Chops 22

Corned Beef and Swiss Cheese Melts..23
Perfect Pork Chop with Spinach and Kale Salad.....................24
Rosemary Pork Chops and Potatoes...25
Hazel Crusted Lamb Rack..26
Tasty Roasted Lamb...27

Chapter 6: Fish and Seafood Recipes..28
Salmon and Dill Dip..28
Salmon And Potato Fishcakes..29
Teriyaki Glazed Halibut Steak..30
Air Fried Crumbed Fish..31
Garlic Ginger Shrimp..32
Lumpy Crab Cakes..33
Parmesan Baked Tilapia..34
Cod Fish Nuggets..35
Cajun Shrimp..36
Island Coconut Shrimp..37

Chapter 7: Chicken and Poultry Recipes..38
Asian Popcorn Chicken..38
Herbal Chicken With Purple Sweet Potato................................39
Honey and Sauce Chicken Wingettes.......................................40
Honey Lime Air-fried Chicken..41
Tasty And Spicy Chicken Jerks..42
Crispy Chicken Fillets..43
Delicious Spicy Drumsticks..44
Spicy Garlic Chicken Nuggets...45
Air Fried Turkey...46
Lemon Turkey Breast..47

Chapter 8: Vegan and Vegetarian Recipes....................................48

Red Bell Pepper and Garlic Mix... 48
Leeks with Sesame Radish... 49
Carrots with Napa Cabbage... 50
Leeks with Parsley Kale.. 51
Endives and Balsamic Cabbage.. 52
Creamy Kale.. 53
Parmesan with Kale... 54
Radish Pomegranate Mix... 55
Leeks with Pine Nuts Okra... 56
Bacon with Lime Cabbage... 57

Chapter 9: Soup, Stew, and Broth Recipes............................. 58
Potato Leek Soup.. 58
Beef Consommé.. 59
Broccoli Cream Soup... 60
Split Pea Bacon Soup... 61
Chilled Melon Soup... 62
Crab and Callaloo Soup... 63
French Onion Soup.. 64
Miso Soup.. 65
Hot Smoked Salmon and Potato Chowder Soup.................... 66
Kale, Sausage with White Bean Soup.. 67

Chapter 10: Beans and Egg Recipes.. 68
Gorgonzola Omelet Roll with Wilted Spinach............................ 68
Egg, Mozzarella, and Baked Tomato inside Phyllo Cups............ 69
Tomato and Brie with Potato Skin and Egg................................ 70
Soft Eggs and Chili-Infused Honey.. 71
Poached Eggs, Horseradish with Corned Beef Brisket............... 72
Sugar Snap Pea with Spinach Salad and Orange........................ 73

Haricots Verts with Roasted Tomato Salad and Roasted Garlic Cream 74
Carrot Salad with Thai-Style Green Bean 75
Beans with Barley Salad 76
Potato, Green Beans and Bacon Salad 77

Chapter 11: Desert and Recipes 78

Coconut Rice Pudding 78
Cheese Babka 79
Cream Coconut Custard Bars 80
Crispy Apple 81
Brown Bites 82
Bacon Blondies 83
Peanuts Butter Pie 84
Jelly Puffs with Chocolate Peanut Butter 85
Chocolate Crème 86
Cheesecake in New York Style 87

Conclusion 88

Description

All-inclusive and mouthwatering recipes perfect for a healthy and pleasurable eating

Would you like to cook **large-sized delectable** meals at a **comfortable** and **swift** pace?

Are you on a hunt for **credible and easy to prepare recipes**?

Search no more. This cookbook is the reward for all your effort. Your journey to **satisfy all your needs** and more has just begun.

The recipes in this cookbook do not merely instruct you on how to combine ingredients; they promise to inform you of the healthiest and affordable dishes for personal, family, and social consumption. The nutritional balance of every dish is taken into consideration for your transformative healthy eating habit and weight loss journey.

Prepare to be blown away with the offerings of this book, which includes:

- An introduction to the Ninja Foodi 10-in-1 XL Pro Air fry Toaster Oven.
- The various functions and components.
- Tips for Usage, Maintenance, and Cleaning.
- 80 scrumptious recipes and their nutritional information.
- FAQs.

Hone your cooking superpower with the Ninja Foodi 10-in-1 XL Pro Air fry Toaster Oven

Press Buy Now?

Introduction

We all want to cook what we love, at our own time, within our budgets and produce the best dishes ever. With the Ninja Foodi 10-in-1 XL Pro Air fry Toaster Oven, this is possible. It is a successful amalgamation of an Air fryer and a toaster convection oven with ten times more power than a regular convection oven. The true surround convection technology is the secret to a juicer, faster, and crispier outcomes all the time.

Make crispier and juicier dishes 30% faster than regular ovens regardless of the larger food quantities you can make due to the extra-large size of the unit. This is just the tip of the iceberg. This unique cooking appliance has many other wonderful attributes for your use.

What are you waiting for? Get your Ninja Foodi 10-in-1 XL Pro Air fry Toaster Oven immediately and start making delicious dishes for yourself and your family right in the confines of your kitchen. It is, after all, a countertop appliance.

Chapter 1: Ninja Foodi 10-in-1 XL Pro Air fry Toaster Oven 101

What is the Ninja Foodi 10-in-1 XL Pro Air fry Toaster Oven?

The Ninja Foodi 10-in-1 XL Pro Air fry Toaster Oven is a compact kitchen equipment blessed with ultimate versatility, multi-functionality, and efficiency. There is room for multi-tasking. You can roast a 5 lb chicken and air fry the vegetable sides all at once. The Ninja Foodi 10-in-1 XL Pro Air fry Toaster Oven has convenience, dependability, and style down pat.

With a stainless steel finish, it is relatively light in weight relative to its capacity (12 lb. chicken fits perfectly with room to spare). Has 1800 watts of power, 130 CFMs airflow, and 450OF maximum temperature level and top to bottom ventilation system make up the super ingredients for short cook time (35 minutes to cook family-sized meals), a 90-second oven preheats time, and a 50% more evenly cooked results.

The Ninja Foodi 10-in-1 XL Pro Air fry Toaster Oven gives 10-in-1 meal options with a 75% cut in fat/calorie content for the ultimate healthy result. Air fry, Air Roast, Whole roast, bake, broil, bagel, toast, pizza, dehydrate, and reheat are the 10 customizable cooking presents available to you.

Functions of the Ninja Foodi 10-in-1 XL Pro Air fry Toaster Oven

The Ninja Foodi 10-in-1 XL Pro Air fry Toaster Oven comprises of a central unit attached to a power cord, a LED screen control panel (displays time, temperature, darkness, shade, start/stop button, preheat, and 10 smart programs), a see-through glass door, four rack positions, and stainless steel accessories; sheet pan, air fry basket, crumb tray, wire rack, and roast tray. The table below outlines the functions of the cooking unit:

Cook settings	Function
Air fry	To make traditionally deep-fried foods like Fried Chicken, French-fries with little to no oil.
Air Roast	Roasts thick proteins and vegetables for a crisp finish and evenly cooked inside.
Whole roast	To simultaneously roast a chicken and side or roast a whole 12 lb chicken or turkey.
Bake	To bake flavored chocolate muffins, chocolate chipped cookies, birthday cakes, and other pastries.
Toast	To toast 9 slices of bread to as dark as you want them.
Bagel	Perfectly toasts nine bagels cut side up.
Pizza	To cook frozen pizza or pizza made from scratch. Can cook two 12-portion pizza comfortably on 2 rack positions.

Broil	To make casserole & broil beef, chicken, and fish.
Dehydrate	To dry meats, fish, veggies to make healthy snacks and for preservation purposes.
Reheat	To warm food gone cold without overcooking or burning it.
Freeze cook cycle	Even when you open the oven door, the cooking display freezes in place, and the cook cycle is unaffected despite the interruption. As a result, no accidental changes can negatively affect the result.
Digital display handle	When you select a cooking program, the correct rack-level lights up, indicating where to place your ingredients appropriately.
360 whole roast	There is no need for flipping food or rotating the cook pans since this feature allows hot air to heat the food from all sides.

Chapter 2: Tips for Usage, Maintenance, and Cleaning

- Always consult the user manual for the recommended cook time and temperature for each smart program to avoid overcooking or burnt food due to the fast cooking technology.
- Use Canola, Avocado, Coconut, Vegetable, and Grapeseed oil to prevent or reduce smoke. Using olive oil, butter, or margarine causes smoking.
- Avoid stacking your ingredients to prevent unevenly cooked food. Arrange the ingredients side by side.
- Hand wash all accessories after every use with warm soapy water, rinse, and then dry thoroughly.
- Use a soft damp cloth/sponge to wipe down the interior and exterior of the main unit and the door. Dry thoroughly with another soft towel. For stubborn stains and food residues, soak the affected accessory overnight in soapy water before washing.
- Your appliance's user manual and inspiration guide are your bibles in the business. Consult them regularly to prevent accidents and mistakes.

Chapter 3: Frequently Asked Questions

- **Does the exterior of the unit also heat up?** Yes! Both the interior and exterior parts become very hot while cooking. Therefore, always use protective covering when handling it.
- **Is it normal for water to seep out during cooking?** Yes! When cooking foods with high moisture content like vegies and frozen bread, it is normal for water to seep out from under the door onto the counter.
- **Is there a default setting?** The unit retains the last input for each function even if the unit switches off. However, to restore the default settings, press the 2 level and light buttons on the control panel for 5 seconds simultaneously.
- **Why does the heating element occasionally go on and off?** The heating element appears to go on and off as the time and temperature for each function adjusts due to varying power levels. It is perfectly normal.
- **What is the warranty policy?** The unit comes with a 60-day money-back guarantee and a 1-year limited warranty. This policy only holds for the unit's non-wearable parts, such as the main unit, control panel, and heating elements.

Chapter 4: Brunch Recipes

Apple Baby Pancake

Apple baby pancake is a Sunday special, sweet and delicious. Another creative way of making pancakes, but the apple transforms the flavor.
Preparation time: 15 minutes
Cooking time: 20 minutes
Serves: 4

Ingredients To Use:

- 3 large eggs, room temperature
- 2 Granny Smith apples, peeled, cored, and sliced
- 4 tbsp butter, divided
- 1 tsp almond extract
- ¾ cup whole milk
- ¼ tsp salt
- 1 tsp cinnamon
- ½ tsp ginger
- 1 Tbsp sugar
- ¾ cup all-purpose flour
- 2 tsp light brown sugar

Step-by-Step Directions to Cook It:

1. Mix all the ingredients in a bowl except the apple, butter, sugar, and cinnamon.
2. To another bowl, add apples, sugar, and cinnamon, toss to coat.
3. Grease the Ninja Foodi XL Pro Air Fry Oven sheet pan with butter
4. Add apple to the bottom of the sheet pan; then top with the batter
5. Preheat the Ninja Foodi XL Pro Air Fry Oven by selecting Bake Mode
6. Adjust temperature to 3500F
7. Open the door and transfer to Ninja Foodi Digital Air Fryer Oven
8. Bake for 10 minutes

Serving suggestions: serve with maple syrup
Preparation and Cooking Tips: Make sure the batter is well mixed
Nutritional value per serving: Calories: 232kcal, Fat: 16g, Carb: 22g, Proteins: 5g

Bacon and Cheese Frittata

Bacon and cheese frittata is incredibly delicious. It will surely brighten up your morning.

Preparation time: 15 minutes
Cooking time: 15 minutes
Serves: 6

Ingredients To Use:

- ½ cup grated cheddar cheese
- 8 slices bacon, chopped and cooked
- 12 large eggs
- 3 Tbsp of milk
- ¼ cup Romano cheese
- Coarse salt, freshly ground pepper, to taste
- Dash of hot sauce

Step-by-Step Directions to Cook It:

1. Add all ingredients to a bowl and mix
2. Pour into the Ninja Foodi XL Pro Air Fry Oven sheet pan
3. Preheat the air fryer by selecting the Bake Mode
4. Adjust temperature to 3700F
5. Open the door and transfer to the Ninja Foodi Digital Air Fryer Oven
6. Bake for 10 minutes

Serving suggestions: serve with a glass of milk

Preparation and Cooking Tips: ensure all ingredients are well mixed

Nutritional value per serving: Calories: 255kcal, Fat: 16g, Carb: 2g, Proteins: 15g

Fluffy Frittata

Just like its name, this recipe is fluffy, soft, and melts in the mouth. It can be easily prepared for breakfast
Preparation time: 15 minutes
Cooking time: 15 minutes
Serves: 4

Ingredients To Use:

- 8 eggs
- 2 Tbsp of whole milk
- 1 bell pepper seeded and diced
- ½ zucchini diced
- 1 Tbsp of butter
- Coarse salt, freshly ground pepper, to taste

Step-by-Step Directions to Cook It:

1. Add all ingredients to a bowl and mix
2. Pour into the Ninja Foodi XL Pro Air Fry Oven sheet pan
3. Preheat the air fryer by selecting the Bake Mode
4. Adjust temperature to 3900F
5. Open the door and transfer to the Ninja Foodi Digital Air Fryer Oven
6. Bake for 15 minutes or until center is no longer jiggly
7. Serve and enjoy

Serving suggestions: serve with a glass of warm milk

Preparation and Cooking Tips: Ensure all the ingredients are well incorporated.

Nutritional value per serving: Calories: 156kcal, Fat: 12g, Carb: 12g, Proteins: 11g

Crispy Cheesy Hash Brown Casserole

This crispy, cheesy hash brown casserole is as delightful as its name. It is creamy and tasty and can quickly become your favorite breakfast

Preparation time: 15 minutes
Cooking time: 20 minutes
Serves: 4

Ingredients To Use:

- 1½ cups shredded hash brown potatoes
- ½ (10.5-oz.) can cream of chicken soup
- ½ cup breadcrumbs
- ½ cup sour cream
- 1 cup shredded cheddar cheese
- ½ tsp. salt
- 2 Tbsp of butter, melted
- 1/3 cup chopped onion
- 2 scallions, finely chopped

Step-by-Step Directions to Cook It:

1. Add all ingredients to a bowl except breadcrumbs and butter. Mix thoroughly
2. Pour into the greased Ninja Foodi XL Pro Air Fry Oven sheet pan
3. Mix butter and breadcrumbs in a bowl, sprinkle over the hash brown mixture
4. Preheat the Ninja Foodi XL Pro Air Fry Oven by selecting Bake Mode
5. Adjust temperature to 3000F and time to 15 minutes
6. Open the door and transfer to the Ninja Foodi Digital Air Fryer Oven
7. Bake until hot and bubbly
8. Serve and enjoy

Serving suggestions: serve with a glass of juice

Preparation and Cooking Tips: allow the ingredients to mix well

Nutritional value per serving: Calories: 212kcal, Fat: 6g, Carb: 12g, Proteins: 5g

Greek Feta Baked Omelet

Greeks foods are known for their delicious taste and spicy aromas. This recipe takes no time and requires little effort.
Preparation time: 15 minutes
Cooking time: 10 minutes
Serves: 4

Ingredients To Use:

- 3 eggs, lightly beaten
- 2 Tbsp of crumbled feta cheese
- 3 Tbsp of frozen leaf spinach, thawed and drained
- 1/8 tsp. oregano
- 6 cherry tomatoes, quartered

Step-by-Step Directions to Cook It:

1. Mix the eggs and other ingredients in a bowl
2. Pour into the greased Ninja Foodi XL Pro Air Fry Oven sheet pan
3. Sprinkle with oregano
4. Preheat the Ninja Foodi XL Pro Air Fry Oven by selecting Bake Mode
5. Adjust temperature to 3300F and time to 10 minutes
6. Open the door and transfer to the Ninja Foodi Digital Air Fryer Oven
7. Remove, Serve and enjoy

Serving suggestions: **serve with toast and a cup of coffee**
Preparation and Cooking Tips: **toss to coat all ingredients**
Nutritional value per serving: **Calories: 190kcal, Fat: 5g, Carb: 2g, Proteins: 15g**

Baked Eggs in Brioche

The baked egg in brioche is nice meal to consume early in the morning. It is easy to prepare with simple steps and ingredients

Preparation time: 10 minutes
Cooking time: 10 minutes
Serves: 4

Ingredients To Use:

- 3 brioche rolls (top cut off and inside scooped out)
- 3 eggs
- 3 slices cheddar Cheese
- 3 Tbsp of butter, melted
- salt and pepper, to taste
- 1 Tbsp of chives

Step-by-Step Directions to Cook It:

1. Brush the inside of the brioche with butter, add a slice of cheese into each brioche
2. Break 1 egg into each brioche, season with salt, chives, and pepper
3. Transfer to the Ninja Foodi XL Pro Air Fry Oven air fryer basket
4. Preheat the Ninja Foodi XL Pro Air Fry Oven by selecting Bake Mode
5. Adjust temperature to 330F and time to 7 minutes
6. Open the door and transfer to the Ninja Foodi Digital Air Fryer Oven
7. Remove, Serve and enjoy

Serving suggestions: Serve with the Orange juice

Preparation and Cooking Tips: season to taste

Nutritional value per serving: Calories: 202kcal, Fat: 6g, Carb: 2g, Proteins: 12g

Parmesan Baked Eggs

This spicy parmesan egg meal is delicious and easy to prepare; don't worry, breakfast will be ready in no time.

Preparation time: 15 minutes
Cooking time: 10 minutes
Serves: 4

Ingredients To Use:

- salt and pepper, as desired
- 6 eggs
- 1 Tbsp of fresh rosemary, minced
- 3 Tbsp of Butter
- 6 tsp of heavy cream
- 1 shallot, grated
- ½ Tbsp of fresh thyme, minced
- 3 Tbsp of grated Parmesan

Step-by-Step Directions to Cook It:

1. Divide all the ingredients evenly into 3 ramekins
2. Sprinkle each ramekin with cheese
3. Preheat the Ninja Foodi XL Pro Air Fry Oven by selecting Bake Mode
4. Adjust temperature to 350F and time to 7 minutes
5. Open the door and transfer to the Ninja Foodi Digital Air Fryer Oven
6. Remove and serve.

Serving suggestions: Season with salt and pepper, sprinkle with cheese

Preparation and Cooking Tips: Cool for 3 minutes before serving.

Nutritional value per serving: Calories: 254kcal, Fat: 9g, Carb: 5g, Proteins: 12g

Sweet-and-Spicy Bacon

This tastes amazing; the spices are well incorporated to give a different but unique taste from ordinary air-fried bacon.

Preparation time: 10 minutes
Cooking time: 10 minutes
Serves: 4

Ingredients To Use:

- 1 lb. thick-cut bacon
- ¼ tsp. black pepper
- 1½ Tbsp of Brown sugar
- ¼ tsp. cayenne pepper

Step-by-Step Directions to Cook It:

1. Mix bacon with all the other ingredients in a bowl
2. Transfer to the Ninja Foodi XL Pro Air Fry Oven air fryer basket
3. Preheat the Ninja Foodi XL Pro Air Fry Oven by selecting Air Fry Mode
4. Adjust temperature to 350F and time to 8 minutes
5. Open the door and transfer to the Ninja Foodi Digital Air Fryer Oven
6. Remove and serve.

Serving suggestions: serve with scrambled egg

Preparation and Cooking Tips: toss to coat all ingredients

Nutritional value per serving: Calories: 236kcal, Fat: 9g, Carb: 2g, Proteins: 14g

Crispy French Fries

This is one of the most straightforward breakfasts to prepare; simple and with easy steps. You can enjoy several sides.

Preparation time: 5 minutes
Cooking time: 15 minutes
Serves: 4

Ingredients To Use:

- 1 large russet potatoes, sliced (1/4-inch thick)
- 1 Tbsp of Canola oil
- ½ tsp. Sea salt
- ½ tsp. black pepper

Step-by-Step Directions to Cook It:

1. Season the potatoes with oil, salt, and pepper.
2. Transfer to the Ninja Foodi XL Pro Air Fry Oven air fryer basket
3. Preheat the Ninja Foodi XL Pro Air Fry Oven by selecting Air Fry Mode
4. Adjust temperature to 390F and time to 10 minutes
5. Open the door and transfer to the Ninja Foodi Digital Air Fryer Oven
6. Remove and serve.

Serving suggestions: serve with tomato Ketchup

Preparation and Cooking Tips: Rinse and drain the Potatoes

Nutritional value per serving: Calories: 210kcal, Fat: 10g, Carb: 12g, Proteins: 3g

Cherry Almond Breakfast Scones

The cherry almond breakfast scones are a delicious pastry that can be eaten for breakfast. Enjoy with any beverage of choice

Preparation time: 15 minutes
Cooking time: 25 minutes
Serves: 4

Ingredients To Use:

- 2 cups all-purpose flour
- 2 tsp baking powder
- ½ cup cold butter
- 3 tbsp brown sugar
- ¾ cup milk
- 1½ cups dried cherries
- Zest of one lemon
- ½ cup chopped almonds
- ½ tsp cinnamon
- 2 Tbsp of Confectioners sugar
- Pinch of salt

Step-by-Step Directions to Cook It:

1. In a bowl, add flour, brown sugar, and salt; combine.
2. Add cold butter, and pinch until to make a crumble dough.
3. Combine with the remaining ingredients except cinnamon, milk, and confectioner's sugar
4. Add the milk and mix gently; do not overwork the dough
5. Pour into a Baking pan that fits into Ninja Foodi XL Pro Air Fry Oven
6. Mix cinnamon and confectioner's sugar, sprinkle on top of the dough
7. Preheat the Ninja Foodi XL Pro Air Fry Oven by selecting Bake Mode
8. Adjust temperature to 375F and time to 25 minutes
9. Open the door and transfer to the Ninja Foodi Digital Air Fryer Oven
10. Remove, Serve and enjoy

Serving suggestions: serve with strawberry jam

Preparation and Cooking Tips: do not overwork the dough

Nutritional value per serving: Calories: 362kcal, Fat: 16g, Carb: 32g, Proteins: 5g

Chapter 5: Beef, Pork, and Lamb Recipes

Dry-Rubbed Flat Iron Steak

This recipe stands out because it is cooked with the Ninja Foodi XL Pro Air-fryer Oven. This brings out a unique flavor.

Preparation time: 5 minutes
Cooking time: 16 minutes
Serves: 4

Ingredients To Use:

- 4 flat iron steaks
- 1 tsp garlic powder
- 1 tsp paprika
- 1 tsp cumin
- 1 tsp onion powder
- ½ tsp coriander
- ½ tsp thyme
- 2 Tbsp olive oil
- ¼ tsp black pepper
- 1 tsp coarse salt

Step-by-Step Directions to Cook It:

1. Combine all the ingredients in a bowl except the steak and oil
2. Season the steak with the mixture and season with oil
3. Transfer to the Ninja Foodi XL Pro Air Fry Oven air fryer basket
4. Preheat the Ninja Foodi XL Pro Air Fry Oven by selecting Broil Mode
5. Adjust temperature to 390F and time to 10 minutes
6. Open the door and transfer to the Ninja Foodi Digital Air Fryer Oven
7. Remove and serve.

Serving suggestions: serve with salad and a glass of wine

Preparation and Cooking Tips: leave the steak to marinate for a few minutes

Nutritional value per serving: Calories: 192kcal, Fat: 6g, Carb: 2g, Proteins: 16g

Steak Seared in Browned Butter

This recipe gives one of the juiciest and tastiest steaks. Besides that, the aroma can attract the entire street to your home

Preparation time: 10 minutes
Cooking time: 20 minutes
Serves: 4

Ingredients To Use:

- 2 (1-lb) steaks, 1 inch thick
- ½ cup beef broth
- ½ cup beef broth
- 1 Tbsp of extra-virgin olive oil
- 3 Tbsp of unsalted butter, divided
- 2 fresh rosemary sprigs
- Salt and freshly ground black pepper, to taste

Step-by-Step Directions to Cook It:

1. Heat oil and one part of butter over medium heat.
2. Season steak with salt and pepper, add in the oil and cook for 2 minutes per side
3. Transfer to a pan that fits into Ninja Foodi XL Pro Air Fry Oven
4. Add the remaining ingredients
5. Preheat the Ninja Foodi XL Pro Air Fry Oven by selecting Air Fry Mode
6. Adjust temperature to 390F and time to 10 minutes
7. Open the door and transfer to the Ninja Foodi Digital Air Fryer Oven
8. Remove and serve.

Serving suggestions: serve with sauce and cooked potatoes

Preparation and Cooking Tips: toss to coat all ingredients

Nutritional value per serving: Calories: 357kcal, Fat: 10g, Carb: 2g, Proteins: 17g

Comforting Red Wine Steak

The perfect recipe for a juicy and tender steak. Prepare for a romantic dinner and enjoy with a side dish of choice.
Preparation time: 5 minutes
Cooking time: 40 minutes
Serves: 2

Ingredients To Use:

- 2 sirloin steaks, trimmed
- Salt and freshly ground black pepper, to taste
- 4 Tbsp extra-virgin olive oil, divided
- 1 lb potatoes, rinsed, halved
- 3 Tbsp shallots, minced
- 2 tsp chopped fresh thyme
- ¾ cup red wine

Step-by-Step Directions to Cook It:

1. Combine all the ingredients in a bowl except potato, toss to coat
2. Season the potatoes with oil, salt, and pepper
3. Transfer the steak and potatoes to the Ninja Foodi XL Pro Air Fry Oven sheet pan
4. Preheat the Ninja Foodi XL Pro Air Fry Oven by selecting Air Fry Mode
5. Adjust temperature to 390F and time to 10 minutes
6. Open the door and transfer to the Ninja Foodi Digital Air Fryer Oven
7. Remove and serve

Serving suggestions: serve with any side dish of choice

Preparation and Cooking Tips: toss to coat all ingredients

Nutritional value per serving: Calories: 162kcal, Fat: 6g, Carb: 12g, Proteins: 15g

Flank Steak Fajitas

Flank steak fajitas are colorful and radiant, but the exquisite quality is the taste. It is has a unique flavor and aroma.

Preparation time: 10 minutes
Cooking time: 20 minutes
Serves: 4

Ingredients To Use:

- 1 lb flank steak
- 3 bell peppers of various colors, washed, seeded, and sliced
- 2 limes, juiced
- ½ cup of soy sauce
- 10 Portobello mushrooms, sliced
- ½ cup honey
- 3 sprigs rosemary
- Salt and pepper, to taste
- 3 cloves garlic, minced
- 2 medium onions, peeled and sliced into rings

Step-by-Step Directions to Cook It:

1. Combine garlic, soy sauce, honey, rosemary, salt and pepper, and lime in a Ziploc
2. Add the steak and marinate for a few minutes
3. Transfer to the Ninja Foodi XL Pro Air Fry Oven air fry basket
4. Preheat the Ninja Foodi XL Pro Air Fry Oven by selecting the Air Fry Mode
5. Adjust temperature to 370°F and time to 20 minutes
6. Open the door and transfer to the Ninja Foodi Digital Air Fryer Oven
7. Meanwhile, heat oil over medium heat, add the remaining ingredients
8. Cook for 6 minutes
9. Remove and serve.

Serving suggestions: serve with sauce and white rice

Preparation and Cooking Tips: drain the marinade

Nutritional value per serving: Calories: 347kcal, Fat: 16g, Carb: 12g, Proteins: 21g

Peppercorn Pork Chops

Peppercorn pork chop is such a tasty and delicious dish that can be served for an early lunch. It comes with simple steps.

Preparation time: 5 minutes
Cooking time: 25 minutes
Serves: 4

Ingredients To Use:

- 4 (10 oz.) pork chops, cut to 1-inch thickness
- 1 (16 oz.) bag frozen green beans
- 1 Tbsp of coarsely crushed black peppercorns
- 2 Tbsp of extra-virgin olive oil
- Salt and freshly ground black pepper, to taste

Step-by-Step Directions to Cook It:

1. Season the pork chops with peppercorn
2. Transfer to the Ninja Foodi XL Pro Air Fry Oven baking sheet
3. Add the remaining ingredients
4. Preheat the Ninja Foodi XL Pro Air Fry Oven by selecting Air Fry Mode
5. Adjust temperature to 350F and time to 20 minutes
6. Open the door and transfer to the Ninja Foodi Digital Air Fryer Oven
7. Remove and serve.

Serving suggestions: serve seasoned with salt and pepper

Preparation and Cooking Tips: toss to coat all ingredients

Nutritional value per serving: Calories: 312kcal, Fat: 8g, Carb: 12g, Proteins: 25g

Corned Beef and Swiss Cheese Melts

Corned beef and swiss cheese melt is a delicious piece of pastry that simply melts in the mouth.

Preparation time: 15 minutes
Cooking time: 12 minutes
Serves: 4

Ingredients To Use:
- 8 oz. corned beef, coarsely chopped
- 1 cup shredded swiss cheese
- 1 Tbsp of Dijon mustard
- 1 tsp. caraway seeds
- 1 (10-oz.) can cream of mushroom soup
- 1 can large biscuit dough

Step-by-Step Directions to Cook It:
1. In a bowl, add all the ingredients except the dough. Thoroughly combine
2. Separate the 8 biscuits and roll out each dough.
3. Spoon the filling in the center of each dough
4. Pull one side of the biscuit over and around the fillings: press together to seal
5. Transfer to the Ninja Foodi XL Pro Air Fry Oven baking sheet
6. Preheat the Ninja Foodi XL Pro Air Fry Oven by selecting bake Mode
7. Adjust temperature to 330F and time to 12 minutes
8. Open the door and transfer to the Ninja Foodi Digital Air Fryer Oven
9. Remove and serve.

Serving suggestions: serve with a glass of milk

Preparation and Cooking Tips: knead the dough gently

Nutritional value per serving: Calories: 312kcal, Fat: 10g, Carb: 22g, Proteins: 15g

Perfect Pork Chop with Spinach and Kale Salad

Pork chop with spinach and kale salad is the perfect combo for a celebratory family dinner or prepared for special guests.

Preparation time: 10 minutes
Cooking time: 20 minutes
Serves: 4

Ingredients To Use:

- 4 pork chops, about 2-inch thick
- ½ cup apple cider vinegar
- 1 Tbsp of whole grain mustard
- 1 cup baby spinach
- 2 Tbsp of Honey
- ½ cup olive oil
- 2½ cups chopped kale leaves
- 1 Granny Smith apple, cut into matchsticks size
- 4 tsp. fresh thyme
- 2 tsp. dried marjoram
- Salt and pepper to taste

Step-by-Step Directions to Cook It:

1. Season steak on both sides with salt, pepper, thyme, and marjoram
2. Transfer to the Ninja Foodi XL Pro Air Fry Oven air fryer basket
3. Preheat the Ninja Foodi XL Pro Air Fry Oven by selecting air fry Mode
4. Adjust temperature to 390F and time to 20 minutes
5. Open the door and transfer to the Ninja Foodi Digital Air Fryer Oven
6. Flip halfway through
7. Meanwhile, combine the rest of the ingredients in a bowl, toss to coat
8. Remove and serve.

Serving suggestions: serve with salad

Preparation and Cooking Tips: toss to coat all ingredients

Nutritional value per serving: Calories: 341kcal, Fat: 11g, Carb: 12g, Proteins: 16g

Rosemary Pork Chops and Potatoes

Rosemary pork chops with potatoes is an excellent way to enjoy lunch. It can also be served for dinner with a glass of wine.

Preparation time: 15 minutes
Cooking time: 20 minutes
Serves: 4

Ingredients To Use:

- 4 boneless pork chops, cut 1 inch thick
- 4 Tbsp of vegetable oil, divided
- 2 Tbsp. chopped fresh rosemary
- 1 tsp. Dried oregano
- 1 Tbsp. chopped garlic
- 1 tsp. dried basil
- 1½ tsp. Salt, divided
- ¾ tsp. ground black pepper, divided
- zest of ½ orange
- 12 small potatoes cut into wedges

Step-by-Step Directions to Cook It:

1. Combine all the ingredients in a bowl. Rub the pork with the mixture
2. In another bowl, add oil, garlic, pepper, and rosemary. Add the potatoes and toss to coat
3. Transfer to the Ninja Foodi XL Pro Air Fry Oven air fryer basket
4. Add the pork chops on top
5. Preheat the Ninja Foodi XL Pro Air Fry Oven by selecting air fry Mode
6. Adjust temperature to 350F and time to 30 minutes
7. Open the door and transfer to the Ninja Foodi Digital Air Fryer Oven
8. Flip halfway. Remove and serve.

Serving suggestions: serve with marinara sauce

Preparation and Cooking Tips: Toss to coat all ingredients

Nutritional value per serving: Calories: 361kcal, Fat: 12g, Carb: 9g, Proteins: 15g

Hazel Crusted Lamb Rack

The recipe produces crispy and delicious meat. The hazelnuts come with a natural flavor and taste; enjoy for lunch.

Preparation time: 10 minutes
Cooking time: 40 minutes
Serves: 4

Ingredients To Use:

- 1 lb. rack of lamb
- 3 oz. hazelnuts, unsalted and finely chopped
- 1 garlic clove, chopped
- 1 Tbsp of chopped fresh rosemary
- 1 Tbsp of olive oil
- 1 egg
- 1 Tbsp of homemade breadcrumbs
- Salt and pepper to taste

Step-by-Step Directions to Cook It:

1. Season the lamb rack with oil, salt, garlic, and pepper
2. In another bowl, add hazelnut, rosemary, and breadcrumbs. Stir well
3. In a third bowl, whisk the egg.
4. Dip the lamb rack in the egg, then in the hazelnut mixture to coat
5. Transfer to the Ninja Foodi XL Pro Air Fry Oven air fryer basket
6. Preheat the Ninja Foodi XL Pro Air Fry Oven by selecting air fry Mode
7. Adjust temperature to 370F and time to 30 minutes
8. Open the door and transfer to the Ninja Foodi Digital Air Fryer Oven
9. Flip halfway. Remove and serve

Serving suggestions: serve with cooked green beans

Preparation and Cooking Tips: toss to coat all ingredients

Nutritional value per serving: Calories: 322kcal, Fat: 14g, Carb: 7g, Proteins: 25g

Tasty Roasted Lamb

This recipe is juicy and flavourful and can be enjoyed with several side dishes.
Preparation time: 60 minutes
Cooking time: 10 minutes
Serves: 4

Ingredients To Use:

- 2½ lbs. lamb leg roast, slits carved
- 1 Tbsp of olive oil
- 2 garlic cloves, sliced into smaller slithers
- 1 Tbsp of dried rosemary
- Cracked Himalayan rock salt to taste
- cracked peppercorns to taste

Step-by-Step Directions to Cook It:

1. Make the cuts in the lamb roast and insert them with garlic. Season with oil
2. Sprinkle the lamb roast with kosher salt, rosemary, and ground black pepper.
3. Place the lamb roast on the Ninja Foodi XL Pro Air Fry Oven air fry basket
4. Preheat the Ninja Foodi XL Pro Air Fry Oven by selecting the Whole roast mode.
5. Adjust the temperature to 3800 F, set time to 75minutes
6. Open the door and transfer to the Ninja Foodi XL Pro Air Fry Oven.
7. Remove and allow to rest
8. Serve and enjoy

Serving suggestions: serve with mushroom sauce

Preparation and Cooking Tips: leave to marinate for a few minutes

Nutritional value per serving: Calories: 242kcal, Fat: 6g, Carb: 12g, Proteins: 25g

Chapter 6: Fish and Seafood Recipes

Salmon and Dill Dip

Steamed salmon and dill dip is the best combo for lunch. It is well spiced with herbs, and the aroma is attractive

Preparation time: 15 minutes
Cooking time: 10 minutes
Serves: 2

Ingredients To Use:

- ¾ lb. of salmon, cut in half
- 6 tsp. of finely chopped dill
- 8 Tbsp of sour cream
- 8 Tbsp of Greek Yogurt
- 2 tsp. of olive oil
- Salt and pepper to taste

Step-by-Step Directions to Cook It:

1. Season the fish with oil, salt, and pepper
2. Transfer to the Ninja Foodi XL Pro Air Fry Oven air fryer basket
3. Preheat the Ninja Foodi XL Pro Air Fry Oven by selecting air fry Mode
4. Adjust temperature to 360F and time to 10 minutes
5. Open the door and transfer to the Ninja Foodi Digital Air Fryer Oven
6. Flip halfway.
7. Meanwhile, in a bowl, add the rest of the ingredients, toss to coat
8. Serve and enjoy

Serving suggestions: serve with dill dip

Preparation and Cooking Tips: mix all the ingredients well

Nutritional value per serving: Calories: 312kcal, Fat: 6g, Carb: 4g, Proteins: 21g

Salmon And Potato Fishcakes

The salmon and potato fish cake is an excellent side dish that can be enjoyed with other meals. You can also prepare it for a small party

Preparation time: 60 minutes
Cooking time: 7 minutes
Serves: 4

Ingredients To Use:

- 14 ounces of potatoes, cooked and mashed
- ½ lb. of salmon, cooked and shredded
- 4 Tbsp of chopped parsley
- 1 ounce of capers
- ¼ cup of flour
- 1 lemon zest
- Salt and peppe, as desired

Step-by-Step Directions to Cook It:

1. Mix all the ingredients except flour, mold into cakes
2. Coat in flour and refrigerate for 1hour
3. Transfer to the Ninja Foodi XL Pro Air Fry Oven sheet pan
4. Spray with cooking oil
5. Preheat the Ninja Foodi XL Pro Air Fry Oven by selecting bake Mode
6. Adjust temperature to 356F and time to 7 minutes
7. Open the door and transfer to the Ninja Foodi Digital Air Fryer Oven
8. Serve and enjoy

Serving suggestions: serve with mint chutney

Preparation and Cooking Tips: ensure all ingredients are well combined

Nutritional value per serving: Calories: 350kcal, Fat: 8g, Carb: 5g, Proteins: 22g

Teriyaki Glazed Halibut Steak

The teriyaki sauce enhances the flavor of the glazed halibut steak. It requires minimum effort to prepare.

Preparation time: 30 minutes
Cooking time: 15 minutes
Serves: 3

Ingredients To Use:

- 1 lb. halibut steak

For the Marinade:

- 2/3 cup low sodium soy sauce
- 2 Tbsp of lime juice
- ¼ cup of orange juice
- ½ cup mirin
- ¼ cup of sugar
- ¼ tsp. ginger ground
- ¼ tsp. crushed red pepper flakes
- 1 garlic clove pressed
- Salt and pepper to taste

Step-by-Step Directions to Cook It:

1. In a bowl, mix all the marinade ingredients. Pour half in a ziplock bag
2. Add the fish and refrigerate for 1hour
3. Remove and transfer to the Ninja Foodi XL Pro Air Fry oven air fry basket
4. Preheat the Ninja Foodi XL Pro Air Fry Oven by selecting air roast Mode
5. Adjust temperature to 390°F and time to 10 minutes
6. Open the door and transfer to the Ninja Foodi Digital Air Fryer Oven
7. Brush with the remaining glaze
8. Serve and enjoy

Serving suggestions: serve with rice and mint chutney

Preparation and Cooking Tips: leave to marinate for a few minutes

Nutritional value per serving: Calories: 378kcal, Fat: 10g, Carb: 5g, Proteins: 25g

Air Fried Crumbed Fish

Air frying fish is always a favorite at any time. Everybody loves a meal that requires little effort and simple steps. Also, it tastes amazing.

Preparation time: 10 minutes
Cooking time: 12 minutes
Serves: 2

Ingredients To Use:

- 4 fish fillets
- 3.5 oz. Breadcrumbs
- 4 Tbsp of vegetable oil
- 1 egg, whisked
- 1 lemon, to serve

Step-by-Step Directions to Cook It:

1. Preheat air fryer to 350°F Ninja Foodi XL Pro Air Fry oven by selecting air fry mode
2. Combine breadcrumbs and stir well until crumbly and loose.
3. Rub the fish fillets with oil, dip in the egg mixture, then in the
4. Dip the fish fillets into the egg, shake off residual then dip in the breadcrumb mixture
5. Transfer to the Ninja Foodi XL Pro Air Fry oven air fry basket
6. Open the door and transfer to the Ninja Foodi Digital Air Fryer Oven
7. Air fry for 12 minutes

Serving suggestions: serve with lemon

Preparation and Cooking Tips: leave to marinate for a few minutes

Nutritional value per serving: Calories: 352kcal, Fat: 6g, Carb: 12g, Proteins: 19g

Garlic Ginger Shrimp

This dish's aroma is unresistable and almost always calls for a second serving. Enjoy as a side dish or main meal.
Preparation time: 15 minutes
Cooking time: 10 minutes
Serves: 4

Ingredients To Use:

- 1 lb. shrimp,
- 2 cloves garlic, chopped
- 2 Tbsp of soy sauce
- 1 tsp. grated ginger
- 2 tsp. fresh-squeezed lime juice
- 2 green onions, chopped
- 1½ Tbsp of sugar
- 3 Tbsp of Butter

Step-by-Step Directions to Cook It:

1. In a bowl, mix all the ingredients.
2. Add the shrimp and refrigerate for 1hour
3. Remove and transfer to the Ninja Foodi XL Pro Air Fry oven air fry basket
4. Spray with cooking oil
5. Preheat the Ninja Foodi XL Pro Air Fry Oven by selecting air fry Mode
6. Adjust temperature to 390°F and time to 10 minutes
7. Open the door and transfer to the Ninja Foodi Digital Air Fryer Oven
8. Flip the shrimps halfway through.
9. Serve and enjoy

Serving suggestions: serve drizzle with the sauce

Preparation and Cooking Tips: leave to marinate for a few minutes

Nutritional value per serving: Calories: 378kcal, Fat: 6g, Carb: 2g, Proteins: 25g

Lumpy Crab Cakes

Crab is known to be delicious, and this recipe gives another creative way of preparing crab. Enjoy as a lunch snack.
Preparation time: 15 minutes
Cooking time: 10 minutes
Serves: 4

Ingredients To Use:

- ½ lb. jumbo lump crabmeat
- 2 slices white bread (crust removed and cut into smaller sizes)
- 2 Tbsp of Mayonnaise
- 2 Tbsp of butter
- ½ tsp. Worcestershire sauce
- 1 egg, beaten
- pinch of salt

Step-by-Step Directions to Cook It:

1. In a bowl, add the crabmeat and the rest of the ingredients except heavy cream
2. Form into four patties
3. Transfer to the Ninja Foodi XL Pro Air Fry oven baking sheet
4. Spray with cooking oil
5. Preheat the Ninja Foodi XL Pro Air Fry Oven by selecting bake Mode
6. Adjust temperature to 370°F and time to 10 minutes
7. Open the door and transfer to the Ninja Foodi Digital Air Fryer Oven
8. Serve and enjoy

Serving suggestions: drizzle with heavy cream and serve
Preparation and Cooking Tips: mix all ingredients until well combined
Nutritional value per serving: Calories: 362kcal, Fat: 13g, Carb: 12g, Proteins: 14g

Parmesan Baked Tilapia

Parmesan baked tilapia is cheesy and full of flavors. It will make a nice lunch or dinner meal, especially on those busy weekdays.

Preparation time: 15 minutes
Cooking time: 10 minutes
Serves: 4

Ingredients To Use:

- 4 tilapia fillets
- 2 cups grated Parmesan cheese
- ¼ cup mayonnaise
- 2 tsp. lemon juice
- ⅛ tsp. cayenne pepper
- 10 ritz crackers, crushed

Step-by-Step Directions to Cook It:

1. In a bowl, mix mayonnaise, cheese, and pepper until well combined
2. Transfer the fish to the Ninja Foodi XL Pro Air Fry oven baking sheet
3. Drizzle with lemon spread the mayonnaise mixture over it
4. Sprinkle with cracker crumbs
5. Preheat the Ninja Foodi XL Pro Air Fry Oven by selecting bake Mode
6. Adjust temperature to 330°F and time to 10 minutes
7. Open the door and transfer to the Ninja Foodi Digital Air Fryer Oven
8. Serve and enjoy

Serving suggestions: sprinkle with cracker crumbs

Preparation and Cooking Tips: ingredients must be well mixed

Nutritional value per serving: Calories: 323kcal, Fat: 13g, Carb: 16g, Proteins: 15g

Cod Fish Nuggets

Codfish nuggets are crispy and crunchy. The perfect meal for lunch and the ideal snack for a night out. Enjoy with ketchup.

Preparation time: 15 minutes
Cooking time: 10 minutes
Serves: 4

Ingredients To Use:

- 1 lb. cod, cut into strips
- The Breading:
- 1 cup all-purpose flour
- ¾ cup panko breadcrumbs
- 2 eggs, beaten
- 2 Tbsp of olive oil
- 1 pinch salt

Step-by-Step Directions to Cook It:

1. In a food processor, add breadcrumbs, oil, and salt. Pulse until smooth
2. Pour the breadcrumb mixture in a bowl, add egg in another bowl
3. Add flour in a third bowl.
4. Dip cod strip in flour, then egg and finally in the breadcrumb mixture
5. Transfer the fish to the Ninja Foodi XL Pro Air Fry oven air fryer basket
6. Preheat the Ninja Foodi XL Pro Air Fry Oven by selecting bake Mode
7. Adjust temperature to 390°F and time to 10 minutes
8. Open the door and transfer to the Ninja Foodi Digital Air Fryer Oven
9. Serve and enjoy

Serving suggestions: **serve with sauce and ketchup**

Preparation and Cooking Tips: **allow ingredients to mix**

Nutritional value per serving: **Calories: 353kcal, Fat: 17g, Carb: 19g, Proteins: 15g**

Cajun Shrimp

Cajun shrimps are as crispy as they come; air fryer the shrimp is a healthy way of preparing the dish; besides, it makes it flavourful.

Preparation time: 5 minutes
Cooking time: 5 minutes
Serves: 4

Ingredients To Use:

- 1 lb.s shrimp
- ¼ tsp. smoked paprika
- ½ tsp. old bay seasoning
- ¼ tsp. cayenne pepper
- 1 Tbsp of olive oil
- 1 pinch salt

Step-by-Step Directions to Cook It:

1. Mix all the ingredients in a bowl, toss to coat
2. Transfer to the Ninja Foodi XL Pro Air Fry oven air fryer basket
3. Preheat the Ninja Foodi XL Pro Air Fry Oven by selecting bake Mode
4. Adjust temperature to 390°F and time to 5 minutes
5. Open the door and transfer to the Ninja Foodi Digital Air Fryer Oven
6. Serve and enjoy

Serving suggestions: **serve over white rice**

Preparation and Cooking Tips: **toss to coat all ingredients**

Nutritional value per serving: **Calories: 391kcal, Fat: 6g, Carb: 9g, Proteins: 15g**

Island Coconut Shrimp

The island coconut shrimp is delicious with its magnified coconut flavor.
Preparation time: 15 minutes
Cooking time: 10 minutes
Serves: 4

Ingredients To Use:

- 18 shrimp, peeled, deveined, and tails left intact
- ¾ cup panko breadcrumbs
- ½ cup shredded unsweetened coconut
- 2 tsp. lime zest
- 1 tsp. salt
- ¼ tsp. black pepper
- 2 eggs

Step-by-Step Directions to Cook It:

1. Mix all the ingredients in a bowl, except egg
2. Add the egg to another bowl. Add the shrimp and toss to coat
3. Remove shrimp and coat in the breadcrumbs mixture
4. Transfer to the Ninja Foodi XL Pro Air Fry oven air fryer basket
5. Drizzle with oil
6. Preheat the Ninja Foodi XL Pro Air Fry Oven by selecting bake Mode
7. Adjust temperature to 370°F and time to 10 minutes
8. Open the door and transfer to the Ninja Foodi Digital Air Fryer Oven
9. Serve and enjoy

Serving suggestions: **serve with any sauce or dippings**

Preparation and Cooking Tips: **toss to coat all ingredients**

Nutritional value per serving: Calories: 381kcal, Fat: 6g, Carb: 12g, Proteins: 25g

Chapter 7: Chicken and Poultry Recipes

Asian Popcorn Chicken

Asian popcorn chicken is as spicy as it is juicy. The spices add flavor to the chicken, creating a unique dish.

Preparation time: 30 minutes
Cooking time: 15 minutes
Serves: 2

Ingredients To Use:

- 1 lb. chicken breast chicken, diced
- 1 clove garlic, medium, minced
- 1 Tbsp of soy sauce
- ¼ tsp. of pepper
- ¼ tsp. of chili pepper
- ¼ t tsp. of five-spice
- ½ tsp. of s corn starch
- 2 green onions, minced
- 1 cup sweet potato starch/corn starch
- 1 egg
- ¼ cup of water

Step-by-Step Directions to Cook It:

1. Mix all the ingredients in a bowl, except the egg, toss to coat
2. Leave to marinate for at least 30 minutes
3. Beat egg in a bowl, cornstarch and mix. Coat chicken with mixture
4. Transfer to the Ninja Foodi XL Pro Air Fry oven air fryer basket
5. Preheat Ninja Foodi XL Pro Air Fry Oven by selecting roast Mode
6. Adjust temperature to 390°F and time to 12 minutes
7. Open door and transfer to the Ninja Foodi Digital Air Fryer Oven
8. Serve and enjoy

Serving suggestions: serve seasoned with salt and pepper

Preparation and Cooking Tips: toss to coat all ingredients

Nutritional value per serving: Calories: 391kcal, Fat: 6g, Carb: 12g, Proteins: 26g

Herbal Chicken With Purple Sweet Potato

Note the combination of this recipe with the purple sweet potato; it creates a fantastic dish that you will love.

Preparation time: 5 minutes
Cooking time: 12 minutes
Serves: 2

Ingredients To Use:

- 1/2 portion of chicken, halved
- 1 tsp. olive
- 1 Tbsp of herbs chicken spices,
- 1 cup of purple sweet potato; brushed clean and pat dry
- 2 cups of salad green

Step-by-Step Directions to Cook It:

1. Season the chicken with olive oil and chicken spices
2. Leave to marinate for at least 30 minutes
3. Transfer to the Ninja Foodi XL Pro Air Fry oven air fryer basket
4. Add the sweet potatoes
5. Preheat the Ninja Foodi XL Pro Air Fry Oven by selecting the Air roast Mode
6. Adjust temperature to 390°F and time to 12 minutes
7. Open the door and transfer to the Ninja Foodi Digital Air Fryer Oven
8. Serve and enjoy

Serving suggestions: Serve with the salad

Preparation and Cooking Tips: toss to coat all ingredients

Nutritional value per serving: Calories: 405kcal, Fat: 6g, Carb: 5g, Proteins: 25g

Honey and Sauce Chicken Wingettes

The sauce is one bonus to this recipe: it brings out the chicken's flavor and boosts the taste.

Preparation time: 40 minutes
Cooking time: 25 minutes
Serves: 6

Ingredients To Use:

- 1 pack of chicken wingettes, rinsed and pat dry
- 1½ Tbsp of honey
- 1½ tbsp of canola oil
- 3 tsp. of oyster sauce
- 3 tsp. of dark soy sauce
- 1 tsp. of light soy sauce
- ½ tsp. of pepper
- Huo Tiao Chinese Wine

Step-by-Step Directions to Cook It:

1. Mix all the ingredients in a bowl, add the chicken, and toss to coat
2. Leave to marinate for at least 30 minutes
3. Transfer to the Ninja Foodi XL Pro Air Fry oven air fryer basket
4. Preheat the Ninja Foodi XL Pro Air Fry Oven by selecting air fry Mode
5. Adjust temperature to 392°F and time to 15 minutes
6. Open the door and transfer to the Ninja Foodi Digital Air Fryer Oven
7. Serve and enjoy

Serving suggestions: serve with sautéed asparagus

Preparation and Cooking Tips: leave to marinate

Nutritional value per serving: Calories: 372kcal, Fat: 6g, Carb: 9g, Proteins: 26g

Honey Lime Air-fried Chicken

This chicken has a sweet, tangy taste that you will love. The marinade enriches the flavor of the chicken, enjoy as a main meal.
Preparation time: 3 hours
Cooking time: 20 minutes
Serves: 4

Ingredients To Use:

- 16 chicken wings; washed & pat dry

Marinade

- 2 tbsps. light soya sauce
- 2 Tbsp of honey
- ¼ tsp. white pepper powder
- 1/2 black pepper, crushed
- 1/2 tsp. sea salt
- 2 Tbsp of lemon juice

Step-by-Step Directions to Cook It:

1. Combine the marinade ingredients, add the chicken, and mix.
2. Leave to marinate for at least 30 minutes
3. Transfer to the Ninja Foodi XL Pro Air Fry oven air fryer basket
4. Preheat the Ninja Foodi XL Pro Air Fry Oven by selecting air fry Mode
5. Adjust temperature to 350°F and time to 12 minutes
6. Open the door and transfer to the Ninja Foodi Digital Air Fryer Oven
7. Serve and enjoy

Serving suggestions: serve with avocado dip

Preparation and Cooking Tips: allow to marinate overnight

Nutritional value per serving: Calories: 393kcal, Fat: 6g, Carb: 10g, Proteins: 27g

Tasty And Spicy Chicken Jerks

Chicken is always everyone's favorite; this can quickly become your Saturday and Sunday special.

Preparation time: 30 minutes
Cooking time: 15 minutes
Serves: 4

Ingredients To Use:

- 30 chicken wings
- 6 tsp. of vegetable oil
- 1 tsp. of white pepper
- 3 tsp. of chopped fresh thyme
- 6 cloves of garlic, finely diced
- 1 tsp. of cinnamon
- 4 green onions, finely chopped
- 8 Tbsp of red wine vinegar
- 2½ ounces of lime juice
- 6 tsp. of soy sauce
- 3 tsp. of grated ginger
- 1 habanera pepper, seeded and finely chopped
- 1 tsp. cayenne pepper
- 6 tsp. of sugar
- 1 tsp. of salt

Step-by-Step Directions to Cook It:

1. Mix all the ingredients in a bowl, toss to coat
2. Leave to marinate for at least 2 hours
3. Transfer to the Ninja Foodi XL Pro Air Fry oven air fryer basket
4. Preheat the Ninja Foodi XL Pro Air Fry Oven by selecting air fry Mode
5. Adjust temperature to 390°F and time to 12 minutes
6. Open the door and transfer to the Ninja Foodi Digital Air Fryer Oven
7. Serve and enjoy

Serving suggestions: serve with tomato sauce and cooked green beans

Preparation and Cooking Tips: leave to marinate

Nutritional value per serving: Calories: 345kcal, Fat: 6g, Carb: 12g, Proteins: 28g

Crispy Chicken Fillets

Crispy chicken fillet is exactly like the name, crispy but also tender. Enjoy with any sauce of choice.

Preparation time: 10 minutes
Cooking time: 15 minutes
Serves: 4

Ingredients To Use:

- 12 ounces of chicken fillets
- 8 Tbsp of breadcrumbs
- 2 Tbsp of vegetable oil
- 2 eggs, whisked
- 4 ounces of flour
- 1 tsp. of ground black pepper
- ½ tsp. salt

Step-by-Step Directions to Cook It:

1. Mix salt, pepper, oil, and breadcrumbs in a bowl
2. Put flour in another bowl and egg in a third bowl
3. Dip chicken in flour, then the egg. Finally, coat with the breadcrumb mixture
4. Transfer to the Ninja Foodi XL Pro Air Fry oven air fryer basket
5. Preheat the Ninja Foodi XL Pro Air Fry Oven by selecting air fry Mode
6. Adjust temperature to 390°F and time to 5 minutes
7. Open the door and transfer to the Ninja Foodi Digital Air Fryer Oven
8. Serve and enjoy

Serving suggestions: serve with salad

Preparation and Cooking Tips: toss to coat all ingredients

Nutritional value per serving: Calories: 389kcal, Fat: 6g, Carb: 14g, Proteins: 17g

Delicious Spicy Drumsticks

Delicious spicy Drumsticks is full of enticing flavors; the spice and herbs are well blended to give you a nice meal.

Preparation time: 5 minutes
Cooking time: 18 minutes
Serves: 4

Ingredients To Use:

- 4 chicken drumsticks
- 6 tsp. of Montreal chicken spices
- 6 tsp. of chicken seasoning
- 6 tsp. of ground black pepper
- 1 tsp. of olive oil
- 1 tsp. of salt

Step-by-Step Directions to Cook It:

1. Mix all the ingredients in a bowl
2. Season chicken with oil
3. Coat the chicken in the spice mixture
4. Transfer to the Ninja Foodi XL Pro Air Fry oven air fryer basket
5. Preheat the Ninja Foodi XL Pro Air Fry Oven by selecting air fry Mode
6. Adjust temperature to 330°F and time to 18 minutes
7. Open the door and transfer to the Ninja Foodi Digital Air Fryer Oven
8. Flip halfway through.
9. Serve and enjoy

Serving suggestions: serve with any sauce

Preparation and Cooking Tips: allow the spice to stick to the chicken

Nutritional value per serving: Calories: 322kcal, Fat: 6g, Carb: 12g, Proteins: 23g

Spicy Garlic Chicken Nuggets

Spicy and tasty are the best words to describe this aromatic dish. Take little time to prepare and with simple steps.
Preparation time: 20 minutes
Cooking time: 20 minutes
Serves: 2

Ingredients To Use:

- 2 chicken breast halves, boneless, skinless,
- ½ lb. of flour
- 1 egg, whisked
- 3 Tbsp of garlic powder
- 1 Tbsp of black pepper
- 1 tsp. of salt

Step-by-Step Directions to Cook It:

1. Mix all the ingredients except the egg in a bowl, put the egg in another bowl
2. Dip the chicken in egg, then coat in the flour mixture
3. Transfer to the Ninja Foodi XL Pro Air Fry oven air fryer basket
4. Preheat the Ninja Foodi XL Pro Air Fry Oven by selecting air fry Mode
5. Adjust temperature to 356°F and time to 20 minutes
6. Open the door and transfer to the Ninja Foodi Digital Air Fryer Oven
7. Flip halfway through
8. Serve and enjoy

Serving suggestions: serve with any sauce or dip

Preparation and Cooking Tips: toss to coat all ingredients

Nutritional value per serving: Calories: 345kcal, Fat: 6g, Carb: 17g, Proteins: 23g

Air Fried Turkey

The air-fried turkey is a crispy and delicious treat on a Sunday afternoon; enjoy your lunch.

Preparation time: 1 hour
Cooking time: 20 minutes
Serves: 4

Ingredients To Use:

- 2 lbs turkey breasts, bone-in skin-on
- 2 tbsps. olive oil
- Coarse sea salt and ground black pepper, to taste
- 1 tsp. fresh basil leaves, chopped
- 2 tbsps. lemon zest, grated

Step-by-Step Directions to Cook It:

1. Season the chicken with oil, salt and pepper
2. Sprinkle with the rest of the ingredients
3. Transfer to the Ninja Foodi XL Pro Air Fry oven air fryer basket
4. Preheat the Ninja Foodi XL Pro Air Fry Oven by selecting the Whole Roast Mode
5. Adjust temperature to 330°F and time to 30 minutes
6. Open the door and transfer to the Ninja Foodi Digital Air Fryer Oven
7. Flip halfway through
8. Serve and enjoy

Serving suggestions: serve with lemon wedges

Preparation and Cooking Tips: toss to coat all ingredients

Nutritional value per serving: Calories: 392kcal, Fat: 12g, Carb: 10g, Proteins: 29g

Lemon Turkey Breast

The lemon turkey breast is a nice and juicy recipe that can be prepared for a celebratory dinner. Enjoy with salad and a glass of wine

Preparation time: 10 minutes
Cooking time: 30 minutes
Serves: 4

Ingredients To Use:

- 4 skin-on boneless turkey breasts
- 1/4 cup olive oil
- 3 Tbsp of garlic, minced
- 2 Tbsp of lemon juice
- 1/3 cup dry white wine
- 1 Tbsp of lemon zest, grated
- 1 1/2 tsp. dried oregano, crushed
- 1 tsp. thyme leaves, minced
- Salt and black pepper
- 1 lemon, sliced

Step-by-Step Directions to Cook It:

1. Combine the marinade ingredients, add the turkey and mix.
2. Leave to marinate for at least 30 minutes
3. Transfer to the Ninja Foodi XL Pro Air Fry oven air fryer basket
4. Preheat the Ninja Foodi XL Pro Air Fry Oven by selecting air fry Mode
5. Adjust temperature to 350°F and time to 30 minutes
6. Open the door and transfer to the Ninja Foodi Digital Air Fryer Oven
7. Serve and enjoy

Nutritional value per serving: Calories: kcal, Fat: g, Carb: g, Proteins: g

Serving suggestions: serve with salad

Preparation and Cooking Tips: leave ingredients to marinate

Nutritional value per serving: Calories: 398kcal, Fat: 8g, Carb: 12g, Proteins: 29g

Chapter 8: Vegan and Vegetarian Recipes

Red Bell Pepper and Garlic Mix

This is a surprisingly satisfying meal. It is perfect for weight loss and can be enjoyed at any time of the day.
Preparation time: 10 minutes
Cooking time: 15 minutes
Serves: 5

Ingredients To Use:

- ½ cup of tomato sauce
- 1 tbsp of parsley
- 1 pound of red bell pepper
- 2 cloves of garlic
- Black pepper and salt
- ½ tsp of curry powder
- 1 tbsp of olive oil

Step-by-Step Directions to Cook It:

1. Grease the baking pan with cooking spray
2. Add the tomato sauce, red bell pepper, garlic, curry powder, pepper, and salt.
3. Place the baking pan in the Ninja Foodi XL Pro Air Fry Oven.
4. Press the bake mode on the air fryer for 15 minutes at 3800F
5. Serve immediately

Serving Suggestion: serve with parsley

Preparation and Cooking Tips: place the baking tray into the appliance appropriately

Nutritional value per serving: Calories: 34kcal, Fat: 0.7g, Carb: 6.5g, Proteins: 1g

Leeks with Sesame Radish

This is a flavorful and tasteful meal. It is easy and very fast to cook. A combination of this recipe makes a healthy meal.

Preparation time: 10 minutes
Cooking time: 16 minutes
Serves: 4

Ingredients To Use:

- 2 tbsp of black sesame seeds
- 2 leeks
- 1 tbsp of chives
- 2 scallions
- 1/3 cup of chicken stock
- 1 tbsp of grated ginger
- ½ pound of radishes

Step-by-Step Directions to Cook It:

1. Mix leeks, radishes, scallions, sesame seeds, chicken stock, ginger, and chives in a bowl.
2. Transfer the mixture to the Ninja Foodi XL Pro Air Fry Oven air fry pan
3. Press the air fry button and set the time for 15 minutes at 3800F
4. Serve

Serving Suggestion: serve with salad cream

Preparation and Cooking Tips: slice the leeks and the radish

Nutritional value per serving: Calories: 20kcal, Fat: 0.5g, Carb: 4g, Proteins: 1g

Carrots with Napa Cabbage

This recipe tastes great and is a fantastic meal for vegetarians.
Preparation time: 10 minutes
Cooking time: 21 minutes
Serves: 4

Ingredients To Use:

- 1 chopped red onion
- 1 shredded napa cabbage
- ½ cup of tomato sauce
- Black pepper and salt
- 2 tbsp of olive oil
- 2 tbsp of sweet paprika
- 2 sliced carrot

Step-by-Step Directions to Cook It:

1. Spray air fryer pan with oil
2. Add red onion, cabbage, tomato sauce, sweet paprika, and carrot.
3. Transfer the pan to the Ninja Foodi XL Pro Air Fry Oven
4. Press the air fry mode on the air fry and set the time for 15 minutes at 3800F
5. Serve immediately

Serving Suggestion: serve with juice

Preparation and Cooking Tips: mix the ingredients well

Nutritional value per serving: Calories: 141kcal, Fat: 4g, Carb: 2g, Proteins: 4g

Leeks with Parsley Kale

This is a very healthy recipe. It has a unique savor. It is suitable for weight loss because it has low calories

Preparation time: 10 minutes
Cooking time: 16 minutes
Serves: 3

Ingredients To Use:

- 1 tbsp of parsley
- 1 pound of torn kale
- ½ cup of tomato sauce
- Black pepper and salt
- 2 tbsp of balsamic vinegar
- 2 sliced leek
- 2 chopped shallots

Step-by-Step Directions to Cook It:

1. Mix all the ingredients in the Ninja Foodi XL Pro Air Fry Oven pan
2. Transfer the pan to the appliance
3. Press the air fry mode and set the temperature to 3800F for 15 minutes
4. Serve immediately

Serving Suggestion: Serve with brown rice

Preparation and Cooking Tips: chop the parsley

Nutritional value per serving: Calories: 101kcal, Fat: 3g, Carb: 4g, Proteins: 5g

Endives and Balsamic Cabbage

This is a delicious and nutritious recipe that gives the body the right energy.
Preparation time: 6 minutes
Cooking time: 16 minutes
Serves: 4

Ingredients To Use:

- 1 tbsp of olive oil
- 1 tbsp of sweet paprika
- 1 shredded green cabbage
- 1 tbsp of balsamic vinegar
- 2 chopped shallots
- Black pepper and salt
- ½ cup of chicken stock
- 2 sliced endives

Step-by-Step Directions to Cook It:

1. Grease a baking pan with cooking oil.
2. Mix cabbage head, endives, shallots, chicken stock, sweet paprika, balsamic vinegar, salt, and pepper in the pan
3. Transfer the pan to the Ninja Foodi XL Pro Air Fry Oven
4. Press the air fry button and set the time to15 minutes at 3800F
5. Serve immediately

Serving Suggestion: serve with soup

Preparation and Cooking Tips: chop the ingredients properly

Nutritional value per serving: Calories: 121kcal, Fat: 3g, Carb: 4g, Proteins: 5g

Creamy Kale

This is a delightful recipe, with a sweet flavor and a fantastic smell. It is great for dinners.
Preparation time: 6 minutes
Cooking time: 16 minutes
Serves: 5

Ingredients To Use:

- 1 tbsp of grated ginger
- Black pepper and salt to taste
- 1 tbsp of lemon juice
- 2 tbsp of chives
- 1 tbsp of grated ginger
- 2 tbsp of olive oil
- 2 tbsp of balsamic vinegar
- 1 clove of garlic
- 1 cup of heavy cream

Step-by-Step Directions to Cook It:

1. Mix all the ingredients in the air fry pan
2. Spray the ingredients with olive oil
3. Put the pan in the Ninja Foodi XL Pro Air Fry Oven
4. Press the air fry mode and set the timer to 14 minutes at 3750F
5. Serve immediately

Serving Suggestion: serve with cream

Preparation and Cooking Tips: chop the chives

Nutritional value per serving: Calories: 131kcal, Fat: 3g, Carb: 4g, Proteins: 3g

Parmesan with Kale

A combination of kale and parmesan gives a healthy and irresistible meal. It is easy and quick to cook.
Preparation time: 6 minutes
Cooking time: 16 minutes
Serves: 4

Ingredients To Use:

- 1 sliced red onion
- 1 tbsp of balsamic vinegar
- ½ cup of chicken stock
- 1 pound of torn kale
- 1 cup of cooked bacon
- Black pepper and salt
- 2 tbsp of parmesan
- 1 tbsp of olive oil

Step-by-Step Directions to Cook It:

1. Mix all the ingredients in the air fry pan
2. Drizzle the ingredients with cooking oil
3. Put the pan in the Ninja Foodi XL Pro Air Fry Oven
4. Press the air fry mode and set the timer to 12 minutes at 3800F
5. Serve immediately

Serving Suggestion: Serve with cheese

Preparation and Cooking Tips: grate the parmesan and chop the bacon

Nutritional value per serving: Calories: 131kcal, Fat: 6g, Carb: 4g, Proteins: 7g

Radish Pomegranate Mix

This is a fantastic recipe. It is preferable for breakfast to give the energy needed for daily work.
Preparation time: 6 minutes
Cooking time: 10 minutes
Serves: 4

Ingredients To Use:

- 2 cloves of garlic
- ¼ cup of pomegranate seeds
- Black pepper and salt
- 1 pound of radishes
- ½ cup of chicken stock
- Black pepper and salt
- 2 tbsp of pomegranate juice

Step-by-Step Directions to Cook It:

1. Combine all the ingredients in a bowl.
2. Grease the air fry pan with cooking spray and add all the ingredients
3. Put the Ninja Foodi XL Pro Air Fry Oven
4. Start the oven and press the air fry mode, and set the time for 8 minutes at 3800F

Serving Suggestion: serve with cream cheese

Preparation and Cooking Tips: cut the radishes into cubes and minced the garlic

Nutritional value per serving: Calories: 134kcal, Fat: 3.5g, Carb: 3g, Proteins: 4g

Leeks with Pine Nuts Okra

This combination is an amazing one because it gives the mouthwatering meal. The procedure below will take you through the beautiful meal journey

Preparation time: 6 minutes
Cooking time: 13 minutes
Serves: 4

Ingredients To Use:

- 1 tbsp of cilantro
- 2 sliced leeks
- 1 cup of tomato sauce
- 1 pound of okra
- ¼ cup of pine nuts
- Black pepper and salt

Step-by-Step Directions to Cook It:

1. Mix all the ingredients in the air fry pan
2. Put the pan in the Ninja Foodi XL Pro Air Fry Oven
3. Start the oven and press the air fry mode, and set the timer for 12 minutes at 3800F
4. Serve immediately

Serving Suggestion: serve with parsley

Preparation and Cooking Tips: get a toasted pine nut and chop the cilantro

Nutritional value per serving: Calories: 145kcal, Fat: 4g, Carb: 5g, Proteins: 4g

Bacon with Lime Cabbage

This is a delightful recipe. It is sweet and very healthy. Lime gives this meal a lasting taste.
Preparation time: 6 minutes
Cooking time: 21 minutes
Serves: 4

Ingredients To Use:

- 1 cup of canned tomatoes
- 4 cups of red cabbage
- 1 lime zest
- 1 tbsp of olive oil
- 2 ounces of bacon
- Black pepper and salt to taste
- ¼ cup of veggie stock

Step-by-Step Directions to Cook It:

1. Spray the cooking pan with olive oil
2. Combine all the ingredients in the pan and toss until well combined
3. Transfer the pan to the Ninja Foodi XL Pro Air Fry Oven
4. Press the air fry mode and set the timer for 20 minutes at 3800F

Serving Suggestion: Serve with brown rice

Preparation and Cooking Tips: crush the tomatoes, cook and crumble the bacon

Nutritional value per serving: Calories: 145kcal, Fat: 4g, Carb: 6g, Proteins: 5g

Chapter 9: Soup, Stew, and Broth Recipes

Potato Leek Soup

Potato leek soup is a very nutritious and delicious soup. It gives the energy needed for the body. Try this amazing soup
Preparation time: 10 minutes
Cooking time: 20 minutes
Serves: 8

Ingredients To Use:

- 7 pounds of peeled and chopped potato
- 6 ounces of butter
- 3g of vegetable stock
- White pepper and salt
- 1 pound of leeks
- 6 cloves of garlic
- ½ tsp of nutmeg

Step-by-Step Directions to Cook It:

1. Put butter in the Ninja Foodi XL Pro Air Fry Oven pan, add garlic, a vegetable stock with potatoes
2. Set the oven to air fry mode for 10 minutes at 1350F
3. Add white pepper, nutmeg, salt, and leek.
4. Cook for another 10 minutes at the same temperature.
5. Allow cooling before serving

Serving Suggestion: serve with rice

Preparation and Cooking Tips: cook the meal at the prescribed temperature

Nutritional value per serving: Calories: 101kcal, Fat: 4g, Carb: 17g, Proteins: 5g

Beef Consommé

This is a fantastic soup for the cold season, especially when the soup is hot. It is tantalizing and also gives the body some warmth.

Preparation time: 10 minutes
Cooking time: 30 minutes
Serves: 17

Ingredients To Use:

- 2 pounds of ground beef
- 2 whole cloves
- ½ tsp of peppercorns
- 12 ounces of diced tomatoes
- 10 egg whites
- 2 bay leaves
- 2 onions, sliced
- 1 pound of mirepoix
- 4 ltr of beef stock or broth
- ½ tsp of dried thyme
- Salt to taste
- 8 parsley stems

Step-by-Step Directions to Cook It:

1. Whisk egg white in a bowl until it foams
2. Add mirepoix, tomatoes, and beef to egg whites.
3. Add onion, beef stock or broth, thyme, bay leaves, peppercorns, parsley stems, and whole clove
4. Put the mix in the Ninja Foodi XL Pro Air Fry Oven pan
5. Set the oven to broil mode, broil for about 30 minutes at 3900F
6. Serve immediately or allow cooling before serving

Serving Suggestion: Serve with brown rice

Preparation and Cooking Tips: strain the soup with cheesecloth to adjust seasonings

Nutritional value per serving: Calories: 21kcal, Fat: 0g, Carb: 1.5g, Proteins: 5g

Broccoli Cream Soup

This soup is a great and healthy one. It is a good cream soup for dinner. You will love the incredible taste

Preparation time: 10 minutes
Cooking time: 25 minutes
Serves: 15

Ingredients To Use:

- 4 ounces of celery
- 4 ounces of whole butter
- 2.8 lt of chicken veloute sauce
- White pepper and salt
- 1 pt of heavy cream
- 2 pounds of broccoli
- Croutons
- 1 pt of chicken sauce
- 8 ounces of onions
- Broccoli florets

Step-by-Step Directions to Cook It:

1. Put the celery and onion in the butter in the Ninja Foodi air fry pan and mix
2. Add broccoli, veloute sauce, and vegetables
3. Put the pan in the Ninja Foodi XL Pro Air Fry Oven
4. Set to broil mode and broil for 15 minutes at 3800F
5. Transfer the soup to the blender after cooking and blend
6. Return it to the oven, add white pepper and salt to taste
7. Broil for some minutes
8. Add cream and serve when it is cool

Serving Suggestion: top with broccoli florets and croutons

Preparation and Cooking Tips: chop the broccoli and dice the onion and celery

Nutritional value per serving: Calories: 252kcal, Fat: 21g, Carb: 14g, Proteins: 8g

Split Pea Bacon Soup

This is a perfect and healthy soup. All the ingredients give the soup an incredible taste.
Preparation time: 10 minutes
Cooking time: 1 hour 15 minutes
Serves: 15

Ingredients To Use:

- 1 pound of diced mirepoix
- 1 pound of split peas
- Pepper and salt
- 2 bay leaves
- 2.8 lt of chicken stock
- ½ tsp of dried thyme
- 2 cloves of garlic
- 1 ½ tsp of ham hocks
- 3 ounces of diced bacon
- ½ tsp of peppercorn
- Croutons

Step-by-Step Directions to Cook It:

1. Mix bacon, garlic, and mirepoix in the air fry pan.
2. Add ham hocks, chicken stock, bay leaves, dried thyme, peppercorn, split peas.
3. Transfer the pan to the Ninja Foodi XL Pro Air Fry Oven
4. Press the broil mode on the oven, broil for about 1 hour at 3800F
5. Transfer the soup to a blender or feed mill and blend
6. Return it to the oven to simmer for some minutes
7. Serve the soup immediately

Serving Suggestion: Serve with croutons

Preparation and Cooking Tips: dice the bacon and the mirepoix. Chop the garlic and rinse the split pea

Nutritional value per serving: Calories: 111kcal, Fat: 5g, Carb: 7g, Proteins: 12g

Chilled Melon Soup

Soup tends to thicken when it is cold. It also has better taste when it is cold. Follow the procedure below and have a great meal

Preparation time: 10 minutes
Cooking time: 30 minutes
Serves: 17

Ingredients To Use:

- 4 pounds of diced honeydew
- 12 ounces of chopped onion
- 6 ounces of olive oil
- Microgreens
- 4 pounds of diced cantaloupe
- 4 tbsp of chopped garlic
- Salt
- 1 lt of buttermilk
- 4 ounces of blanched almond
- 30 ml of balsamic vinegar
- 4 tbsp of honey
- 4 tbsp of chopped basil leaves
- Crispy prosciutto chips

Step-by-Step Directions to Cook It:

1. Put oil in the air fry pan, add almond, garlic, melon, and onion
2. Put the pan inside Ninja Foodi XL Pro Air Fry Oven, press the broil button on the oven
3. Broil for about 10 minutes at 3800F
4. Add buttermilk, nectar, cook for another 15 minutes
5. Transfer the soup to a blender or feed mill and blend
6. Add salt to taste, put the soup in the refrigerator
7. Serve when it is chilled

Serving Suggestion: serve with crisp prosciutto chips

Preparation and Cooking Tips: peel the garlic, onion, honeydew, cantaloupe. Chop the basil leaves

Nutritional value per serving: Calories: 181kcal, Fat: 11g, Carb: 24g, Proteins: 5g

Crab and Callaloo Soup

Crab and callaloo make an excellent combination for soup. This soup is good for summer. It can be make for a special family gathering.
Preparation time: 10 minutes
Cooking time: 35 minutes
Serves: 19

Ingredients To Use:

- 4 cloves of garlic
- 8 ounces of callaloo
- 1 lt of milk
- 2 pound of crab meat
- 2 ounces of olive oil
- 2 tsp of black pepper
- 1 pound of fresh pumpkin
- 720 ml of coconut milk
- 12 ounces of green onion
- 2 tbsp of salt
- 1 pound of onion

Step-by-Step Directions to Cook It:

1. Rinse the callaloo and remove the stem, chop it
2. Put oil, onion, garlic, green onion
3. Put the pan in the Ninja Foodi XL Pro Air Fry Oven, press the air fry mode
4. Air fry for 2 minutes at 3500F
5. Add milk, callaloo, coconut milk, pepper, pumpkin, and salt
6. Cook for another 30 minutes at the same temperature
7. Transfer the soup to a blender and blend
8. Adjust the seasoning to ensure the taste
9. Serve immediately

Serving Suggestion: serve with parmesan

Preparation and Cooking Tips: dice the onion and the fresh pumpkin

Nutritional value per serving: Calories: 191kcal, Fat: 12g, Carb: 12g, Proteins: 13g

French Onion Soup

This is an exceptional soup. It is uncommon because not everybody likes onion. It is a tremendous and nutritional soup

Preparation time: 10 minutes
Cooking time: 30 minutes
Serves: 18

Ingredients To Use:

- ½ ounces of fresh thyme
- 8 pounds of thinly sliced yellow onion
- 8 ounces of cherry
- 2.8 lt of beef stock
- Pepper and salt
- 8 ounces of butter
- Gruyere cheese
- French bread slices
- 1.9 lt of chicken stock

Step-by-Step Directions to Cook It:

1. Put butter and onion in the air fry pan
2. Put the pan in the Ninja Foodi XL Pro Air Fry Oven, press the air fry button and saute for 5 minutes at 3600F
3. Add beef stock and cook for about 5 minutes at the same temperature
4. Add chicken stock, thyme, salt, pepper, and sherry, air fry for another 20 minutes
5. Adjust the seasoning if it is not enough
6. Serve when it is cool

Serving Suggestion: Serve with French bread slices, and top with gruyere cheese

Preparation and Cooking Tips: grate the cheese, mix the ingredients in the right proportion

Nutritional value per serving: Calories: 281kcal, Fat: 13g, Carb: 35g, Proteins: 10g

Miso Soup

This is a traditional Japanese soup. It is a soup with a good flavor and pleasant aroma. The procedure below will give the best soup
Preparation time: 10 minutes
Cooking time: 20 minutes
Serves: 13

Ingredients To Use:

- 1 pt of miso paste
- ½ ounce of dried wakame
- 1 ounce of green onion
- 3.1 ltr of dashi
- 1 pound of silken tofu
- 960ml of shiitake mushroom

Step-by-Step Directions to Cook It:

1. Cut the stem and leaves of wakame and soak in hot water for about 30 minutes
2. Drain and rinse with cold water
3. Broil the mushroom with water in the Ninja Foodi XL Pro Air Fry Oven at 3000F for 5 minutes
4. Remove and drain from water
5. Put dashi, onion, and miso in the air fry pan, broil for 10 minutes
6. Serve the soup

Serving Suggestion: serve with tofu, mushroom, and wakame

Preparation and Cooking Tips: dice the silken tofu

Nutritional value per serving: Calories: 131kcal, Fat: 2g, Carb: 28g, Proteins: 4g

Hot Smoked Salmon and Potato Chowder Soup

A combination of these recipes give the best soup you have long for. It is easy to make and does not take time
Preparation time: 10 minutes
Cooking time: 10 minutes
Serves: 17

Ingredients To Use:

- 1.9 lt of chicken stock
- 8 ounces of prosciutto ham
- Pepper and salt
- 2 tsp of dried dill
- 10 ounces of heavy cream
- 4 ounces of clarified butter
- 6 ounces of diced smoked salmon
- 8 ounces of onion
- 3 pounds of Yukon gold potatoes
- Pepper and salt
- Fresh dill sprigs
- 3 ounces of flour

Step-by-Step Directions to Cook It:

1. Put butter, onion, and prosciutto in a pan. Add flour
2. Put the pan in the Ninja Foodi air fryer oven, set the oven to broil mode
3. Cook for 5 minutes at 3500F
4. Add chicken stock, salmon, thyme, dill, and cream.
5. Cook for another 10 minutes at the same temperature, adjust the seasoning
6. Serve immediately or allow cooling before serving

Serving Suggestion: serve with dill sprigs

Preparation and Cooking Tips: dice the onion and the potatoes

Nutritional value per serving: Calories: 271kcal, Fat: 15g, Carb: 17g, Proteins: 20g

Kale, Sausage with White Bean Soup

The combination of this recipe gives excellent soup. It is a good soup for dinner. Have an incredible soup journey

Preparation time: 10 minutes
Cooking time: 20 minutes
Serves: 18

Ingredients To Use:

- 1 pound of plum tomatoes
- 1.9 lt of chicken stock
- 2 tbsp of minced garlic
- 4 ounces of kale
- Grated parmesan
- 1 pound of Italian pork sausage
- 2 tbsp of salt
- 2 tbsp of olive oil
- Croutons
- 480ml of white wine
- 1 ½ pound of cooked white beans
- 1 tsp of pepper
- 1 pound of diced onion

Step-by-Step Directions to Cook It:

1. Put the oil and pork sausage in the pan
2. Put the pan in the Ninja Foodi air fryer oven, press the roast mode, and roast for 5 minutes at 3800F
3. Add garlic, pepper, wine, onion, tomatoes, salt, white bean, and kale
4. Cook for another 15 minutes at the same temperature
5. Serve immediately

Serving Suggestion: serve with parmesan, garlic croutons, and red pepper

Preparation and Cooking Tips: remove the kale ribs, grated parmesan

Nutritional value per serving: Calories: 141kcal, Fat: 6g, Carb: 15g, Proteins: 9g

Chapter 10: Beans and Egg Recipes

Gorgonzola Omelet Roll with Wilted Spinach

Omelet roll garnished gorgonzola and wilted spinach gives good savor and great taste. This recipe is good for breakfast

Preparation time: 10 minutes
Cooking time: 20 minutes
Serves: 6

Ingredients To Use:
- 2 tbsp of olive oil
- 6 big eggs
- ½ cup of crumbled gorgonzola cheese
- ¼ cup of unsalted butter
- 1 tsp of minced garlic
- 1 cup of whole milk
- 12 ounces of baby spinach
- ½ cup of all-purpose flour
- 2 tsp of parsley, chopped

Step-by-Step Directions to Cook It:
1. Mix eggs, butter, milk, parsley, and flour in a bowl until it is foamy and well mixed.
2. Add parsley
3. Pour the mixture into a greased pan
4. Put the pan in the Ninja Foodi XL Pro Air Fry Oven, press the bake mode on the oven
5. Bake for about 18 minutes at 4000F.
6. Add spinach and garlic, bake for another 2 minutes at the same temperature
7. Put the cheese on it and allow to melt
8. Slice the omelet roll and serve

Serving Suggestion: Serve with coffee

Preparation and Cooking Tips: remove the baby spinach stem and rinse

Nutritional value per serving: Calories: 187kcal, Fat: 13g, Carb: 3g, Proteins: 17g

Egg, Mozzarella, and Baked Tomato inside Phyllo Cups

The is an exotic presentation of baked tomato with eggs and Mozzarella. It is sweet and memorable.
Preparation time: 5 minutes
Cooking time: 15 minutes
Serves: 6

Ingredients To Use:

- 6 big eggs
- 5 sheets of phyllo
- ½ cup of shredded mozzarella cheese
- 2 tsp of chopped chives
- 4 tbsp of unsalted butter
- 1 tbsp of chopped shallots
- 3 plum tomatoes

Step-by-Step Directions to Cook It:

1. Drizzle muffin pan with 2 tbsp of butter
2. Rub ¼ phyllo sheet with butter, place the phyllo sheet in each other and press it in the muffin cups
3. Ensure each muffin cup has layers of phyllo sheet rubbed with butter
4. Put the muffin pan in the Ninja Foodi XL Pro Air Fry Oven
5. Bake for 10 minutes at 3750F, add the shallot, and bake for another 2 minutes
6. Add the eggs to the cup and bake for 2 minutes, add 2 slices of tomatoes, top with mozzarella cheese
7. Bake for another 5 minutes until the cheese melts.
8. Serve immediately

Serving Suggestion: serve with chives

Preparation and Cooking Tips: chop the shallots and the chives

Nutritional value per serving: Calories: 524kcal, Fat: 23g, Carb: 64g, Proteins: 33g

Tomato and Brie with Potato Skin and Egg

This is a fantastic combination. It has an incredible flavor and a mouthwatering taste.

Preparation time: 10 minutes
Cooking time: 1 hour 30 minutes
Serves: 6

Ingredients To Use:

- 1 tbsp of butter
- 3 big baking potatoes
- 2 tbsp of flat-leaf parsley, chopped
- ½ tsp of salt
- 3 big tomatoes
- 6 ounces of brie
- ½ tsp of salt
- ½ tsp of ground pepper

Step-by-Step Directions to Cook It:

1. Prick potatoes and put it in the baking pan
2. Put the baking pan in the Ninja Foodi XL Pro Air Fry Oven, press the baking button
3. Bake for 1 hour at 3750F
4. Remove the potato skin and return to oven, bake for another 5 minutes
5. Mix salt, pepper, and egg in a bowl
6. Heat the egg in the air fryer oven for 2 minutes at the same temperature
7. Put the egg mix on the potato skins, add tomato slices, add brie and bake for 6 minutes at the same temperature
8. Serve immediately

Serving Suggestion: serve with parsley

Preparation and Cooking Tips: chop the flat-leaf parsley, thinly slice the brie

Nutritional value per serving: Calories: 210kcal, Fat: 18g, Carb: 9g, Proteins: 6g

Soft Eggs and Chili-Infused Honey

Honey gives a meal a sweet and lasting flavor. It also adds nutrients to the meal. This is an irresistible breakfast

Preparation time: 5 minutes
Cooking time: 10 minutes
Serves: 6

Ingredients To Use:

- 1 cup of honey
- 6 big eggs
- 8 dried chili peppers
- Pepper and salt to taste

Step-by-Step Directions to Cook It:

1. Mix the chili pepper and ½ cup honey in a bowl
2. Put the egg in the air fry pan and add water
3. Put the pan in the Ninja Foodi XL Pro Air Fry Oven, press the broil button
4. Soft cook for about 10 minutes at 3000F
5. Remove the shell and cut into two halves
6. Top with the honey mixture and serve

Serving Suggestion: Serve with honey

Preparation and Cooking Tips: the egg should not cook too hard

Nutritional value per serving: Calories: 79kcal, Fat: 5.6g, Carb: 1.5g, Proteins: 7g

Poached Eggs, Horseradish with Corned Beef Brisket

This recipe needs the right proportion of each ingredient, which is also listed below. Have a great meal.

Preparation time: 10 minutes
Cooking time: 20 minutes
Serves: 6

Ingredients To Use:

- 1/2 cup of chopped onion
- 4 white potatoes
- 1 tbsp of unsalted butter
- 1 tbsp of chopped chives
- 6 big eggs
- 1 tbsp of salt
- 1 cup of crème Fraiche
- 12 thinly sliced beef brisket
- ¼ cup of fresh horseradish
- 3 tbsp of olive oil

Step-by-Step Directions to Cook It:

1. Put the potatoes in a pan, add water and boil over medium heat for 5 minutes
2. Grease the Ninja Foodi XL Pro Air Fry Oven pan with oil
3. Put cooked potatoes, onion, corn beef.
4. Bake at 3500F for 4 minutes in the Ninja Foodi XL Pro Air Fry Oven
5. Prepare to poach eggs by cracking the eggs into ramekins
6. Trim the edge of the egg white and use a spoon to hold the eggs inside hot water to ensure that it does not stick to the button
7. Allow to soft cook for 2 minutes ensuring the yolk is not cooked or cook for 3 minutes depending on how you want the yolk done
8. Remove the eggs and open it on plates
9. Mix crème Fraiche with horseradish, divide it on the poach eggs
10. Serve with potato mix

Serving Suggestion: serve with chives on top

Preparation and Cooking Tips: coarsely chop the corned beef

Nutritional value per serving: Calories: 421kcal, Fat: 13g, Carb: 48g, Proteins: 29g

Sugar Snap Pea with Spinach Salad and Orange

This meal is a good winter meal. It is an exquisite recipe that you absolutely need to try.

Preparation time: 10 minutes
Cooking time: 1½ hour
Serves: 4

Ingredients To Use:

- 1 pound of sugar snap peas
- 3 scallions
- Black pepper and salt
- ½ pound of baby spinach
- 1 citrus mint vinaigrette
- 2 oranges

Step-by-Step Directions to Cook It:

1. Put water and sugar snap peas in a pan
2. Put the pan in the Ninja Foodi XL Pro Air Fry Oven.
3. Press the broil button and cook for 1 hour at 4500F or until it is bright green
4. Drain the peas when done, add salt, pepper orange, spinach, scallion, and vinaigrette
5. Serve immediately

Serving Suggestion: serve with parsley

Preparation and Cooking Tips: make sure the pea changes to exquisite bright green before removing from the oven

Nutritional value per serving: Calories: 120kcal, Fat: 9g, Carb: 7g, Proteins: 3g

Haricots Verts with Roasted Tomato Salad and Roasted Garlic Cream

This is a nutritional and perfect meal for every season. The beans are available in every food store

Preparation time: 10 minutes
Cooking time: 30 minutes
Serves: 5

Ingredients To Use:

- Fresh chives
- 1 tbsp of olive oil
- 1/3 cup of heavy cream
- Lettuce leaves
- 1 pound of haricot verts
- 2 heads of roasted garlic
- 1 tsp of wine vinegar
- Black pepper
- 1/3 cup of greek-style yogurt
- 10 big tomatoes
- Salt

Step-by-Step Directions to Cook It:

1. Put haricot verts into boiling water until the color brightens
2. Drain and rinse the haricot and allow to chill
3. Grease the air fry pan with 1 tsp of oil, add tomatoes, salt
4. Put the pan in the Ninja Foodi XL Pro Air Fry Oven
5. With the Roast Mode, cook for 20 minutes at 4500F
6. Mix the heavy cream, mashed roasted garlic, wine vinegar, and yogurt in a bowl
7. Add the roasted tomato and the chilled haricots verts, sprinkle salt and black pepper to taste
8. Pour garlic cream over it and add lettuce leaves to each plate
9. Serve

Serving Suggestion: serve with chives

Preparation and Cooking Tips: make sure the pea color brightens

Nutritional value per serving: Calories: 90kcal, Fat: 7g, Carb: 8g, Proteins: 3g

Carrot Salad with Thai-Style Green Bean

This can be eaten with lime and peanuts. Lime gives it a lasting flavor. This recipe is one of the best ways to make green beans
Preparation time: 5 minutes
Cooking time: 5 minutes
Serves: 4

Ingredients To Use:

- 3 scallions
- 1 Thai-style dressing
- 3 grated carrots
- ¼ cup of chopped peanuts
- 5 cups of Asian salad greens
- 3 cups of thinly sliced Chinese cabbage
- ¾ pound of cooked green beans
- 4 hot Thai pepper

Step-by-Step Directions to Cook It:

1. Mix all the ingredients in a bowl except peanuts
2. Pour the mixture into the air fry pan
3. Transfer the pan to the Ninja Foodi XL Pro Air Fry Oven
4. Cook in Bake Mode for 5 minutes at 4500F
5. Serve immediately

Serving Suggestion: serve with peanuts

Preparation and Cooking Tips: mix the ingredients well

Nutritional value per serving: Calories: 31kcal, Fat: 0.5g, Carb: 7g, Proteins: 2g

Beans with Barley Salad

This is a beautiful and healthy meal. This salad recipe is a good meal for dinner. Follow the procedure below and have the best meal

Preparation time: 10 minutes
Cooking time: 20 minutes
Serves: 7

Ingredients To Use:

- ½ pound of cooked and frozen green beans
- 1 cup of frozen peas
- 3 scallion
- 1 cucumber
- 2 lemon
- 4 cups of chilled pearled barley
- ½ cup of minced fresh herbs
- Red and yellow cherry pepper
- 3 chopped carrot
- Crumbled feta
- Lettuce leaves
- Black pepper and salt
- 1 ½ cup of canned chickpeas
- 3 tbsp of olive oil

Step-by-Step Directions to Cook It:

1. Put the peas in a colander
2. Broil the carrots for 2 minutes at 350°F and pour it on the peas, rinse them with cold water
3. Mix peas, chickpeas, scallion, herbs, green beans, cucumber, barley in the air fry pan and toss
4. Spray with oil, squeeze lemon over it. Add salt and pepper
5. Put it in the Ninja Foodi XL Pro Air Fry Oven, Roast for about 3-5 minutes at 3000F
6. Serve with cherry tomatoes and crumbled feta

Serving Suggestion: serve with lettuce leaves

Preparation and Cooking Tips: mix the ingredients well

Nutritional value per serving: Calories: 338kcal, Fat: 16g, Carb: 44g, Proteins: 10g

Potato, Green Beans and Bacon Salad

This meal is one of its kind. It gives a sweet memory of how amazing it is. A healthy and perfect meal for the family!
Preparation time: 10 minutes
Cooking time: 15 minutes
Serves: 6

Ingredients To Use:

- 1/3 cup of white wine vinegar
- 6 slices of bacon
- 4 scallions
- Black pepper and salt
- 2 tbsp of unbleached white flour
- ¾ pound of freshly cooked green beans
- 2 tbsp of finely minced parsley
- 2 pounds of steamed potatoes
- 3 tbsp of sugar

Step-by-Step Directions to Cook It:

1. Cook the bacon in the Ninja Foodi XL Pro Air Fry Oven for 10 minutes at 4000F
2. Drain and crumble the bacon
3. Put 3 tbsp of bacon fat in another bowl
4. Add flour to the remaining bacon fat, add vinegar, sugar, and 1/3 cup of water
5. Add green beans, potatoes, and vegetables.
6. Put the mixture in the Ninja Foodi XL Pro Air Fry Oven and broil for 15 minutes at 4000F
7. Add pepper and salt, serve

Serving Suggestion: serve with parsley and crumbled bacon
Preparation and Cooking Tips: cook the potato until the water is thick
Nutritional value per serving: Calories: 200kcal, Fat: 10g, Carb: 22g, Proteins: 10g

Chapter 11: Desert and Recipes

Coconut Rice Pudding

Coconut rice pudding is an excellent dessert. It is one of the best desserts available and it will give you a sweet sensation
Preparation time: 6 minutes
Cooking time: 15 minutes
Serves: 6

Ingredients To Use:

- 1 cup of milk
- ¾ cup of Arborio rice
- ¾ cup of granulated sugar
- 1 can of unsweetened full-fat coconut oil
- 1 cup of water
- ½ tsp of vanilla extract

Step-by-Step Directions to Cook It:

1. Rinse the rice well
2. Put the rice in the air fry pan, add water, milk, vanilla, coconut milk.
3. Place the pan in the Ninja Foodi XL Pro Air Fry Oven
4. Set the air fry to broil mode
5. Cook for 15 minutes at 4000F
6. Serve immediately

Serving Suggestion: serve with soup

Preparation and Cooking Tips: rinse the rice well

Nutritional value per serving: Calories: 365kcal, Fat: 20g, Carb: 51g, Proteins: 6g

Cheese Babka

This cheese babka is a great dessert. It is sweet and delightful. Follow the recipe below and have the best meal

Preparation time: 25 minutes
Cooking time: 35 minutes
Serves: 8

Ingredients To Use:

- 2 cups, 1 tbsp of all-purpose flour
- 1 packet of active yeast
- 3 tbsp of unsalted butter
- ¼ cup, ¼ tsp of granulated sugar
- 2 big eggs
- ½ tsp of kosher salt
- ¼ cup of warm water
- Cooking spray
- 1 tbsp of sour cream
- 8 ounces of cream cheese
- 1 lemon zest
- ½ tsp of vanilla extract
- 3 tbsp of water

Step-by-Step Directions to Cook It:

1. Mix warm water, ¼ tsp of sugar, and yeast in a bowl.
2. Put egg, milk, ¼ cup of sugar, and butter in a mixer, add yeast mixture and flour
3. Whisk the ingredients well
4. Spray cooking pan with cooking spray
5. Pour the dough into the cooking pan, cover with plastic wrap and leave for about an hour to increase in size
6. Remove the plastic wrap, spread the cream cheese on it, add sugar, sour cream, 1 tbsp of all-purpose flour, vanilla extract, lemon zest.
7. Whisk egg and 1 tsp of water in a bowl
8. Brush the dough with egg wash
9. Place the pan in the lower level in the Ninja Foodi XL Pro Air Fry Oven
10. Press the bake mode for 30 minutes at 3250F
11. Serve immediately

Serving Suggestion: serve with cream
Preparation and Cooking Tips: cover the dough to wrap to double the size
Nutritional value per serving: Calories: 327kcal, Fat: 17g, Carb: 40g, Proteins: 8g

Cream Coconut Custard Bars

This dessert is creamy and beautiful. The bars are good desserts after lunch.
Preparation time: 10 minutes
Cooking time: 21 minutes
Serves: 8

Ingredients To Use:

- 1 cup of milk
- 2 tbsp of granulated sugar
- ½ cup of chopped almonds
- 6 tbsp of unsalted butter
- 4 tbsp of finely chopped chocolate
- Cooking spray
- 1 ¼ cups of all-purpose flour
- ½ cup of unsweetened shredded coconut
- 1 cup of heavy cream
- 1 package of instant vanilla pudding

Step-by-Step Directions to Cook It:

1. Mix flour, ¼ cup of almond, butter, sugar, and ¼ cup of coconut in a bowl, stir well
2. Pour the dough into Ninja Foodi XL Pro Air Fry Oven pan
3. Spray the pan with cooking oil
4. Pour the remaining coconut and ¼ cup of almond on the pan
5. Press the bake mode on the air fry oven for 20 minutes at 350°F
6. Cut into wedges and serve

Serving Suggestion: serve with chocolates

Preparation and Cooking Tips: use a mixer to mix the ingredients well

Nutritional value per serving: Calories: 477kcal, Fat: 34g, Carb: 40g, Proteins: 7g

Crispy Apple

This is a fast and easy dessert to make. It can be eaten instead of apple pie. It is a healthy snack.
Preparation time: 15 minutes
Cooking time: 22 minutes
Serves: 8

Ingredients To Use:
- ½ cup of all-purpose flour
- 2 tsp of cinnamon
- 4 apples
- 1/3 cup of unsalted butter
- 1 tsp of squeezed lemon juice
- 2/3 cup of brown sugar
- 1 tbsp of cornstarch
- ½ cup of rolled oats
- ½ cup, 1 tbsp of water
- 5 tbsp of granulated sugar

Step-by-Step Directions to Cook It:
1. Put the cubed apples in the air fry pan
2. Mix lemon juice, cornstarch, 3 tbsp of granulated sugar, 1 tsp of cinnamon, and 1 tbsp of water.
3. Pour the mixture over the cubed apples
4. Put the pan in the Ninja Foodi XL Pro Air Fry Oven, set the air fry to bake mode for 15 minutes at 3750F
5. Mix the oats, butter, flour, 1 tsp of cinnamon, 2 tbsp of granulated sugar, and brown sugar in a bowl.
6. Pour the crispy mix over the apple, bake for another 5 minutes
7. Serve immediately

Serving Suggestion: serve with juice
Preparation and Cooking Tips: mix the ingredients thoroughly
Nutritional value per serving: Calories: 260kcal, Fat: 10g, Carb: 47g, Proteins: 3g

Brown Bites

Brown bites are unique and delicious. It has a mouthwatering taste and lasting flavor. It is a night out snack

Preparation time: 10 minutes
Cooking time: 45 minutes
Serves: 9

Ingredients To Use:

- 1 box of brownie mix
- Carmel sauce
- Cooking spray
- Confectioners' sugar

Step-by-Step Directions to Cook It:

1. In a bowl, mix the brownie mix according to the instruction
2. Scoop the brownie in a small mold to the air fry pan
3. Spray the pan with cooking spray
4. Put the pan inside Ninja Foodi XL Pro Air Fry Oven
5. Press the bake mode for 45 minutes at 375°F
6. Serve immediately

Serving Suggestion: serve with caramel sauce and confectioners' sugar

Preparation and Cooking Tips: mix the brownie according to instruction

Nutritional value per serving: Calories: 290kcal, Fat: 6g, Carb: 45g, Proteins: 3g

Bacon Blondies

Bacon blondies are incredible snacks. It is easy to cook and very fast. This is a fantastic snack to try out

Preparation time: 15 minutes
Cooking time: 35 minutes
Serves: 6

Ingredients To Use:

- 2 cups of all-purpose flour
- 6 slices of uncooked bacon
- 1 cup of brown sugar
- 1 ½ cups of unsalted butter
- Ice cream

Step-by-Step Directions to Cook It:

1. Drizzle the Ninja Foodi air fry pan with butter
2. Place the bacon in the pan, put the pan in the Ninja Foodi XL Pro Air Fry Oven
3. Set the oven to Roast mode for 5 minutes at 4000F
4. Transfer the bacon to a dish
5. Use the mixer to mix brown sugar and butter in a bowl, add flour, and whisk
6. Place the bacon in the dough and coat
7. Put the dough containing bacon in the air fry pan
8. Put the air fry pan back to the oven, select roast mode for 25 minutes at 3500F
9. Serve after cooling

Serving Suggestion: serve with ice cream

Preparation and Cooking Tips: mix the ingredients well

Nutritional value per serving: Calories: 770kcal, Fat: 55g, Carb: 61g, Proteins: 40g

Peanuts Butter Pie

Peanuts butter pie is a sweet and fantastic pie. It is compelling and extraordinary. It is a healthy pie.
Preparation time: 11 minutes
Cooking time: 30 minutes
Serves: 10

Ingredients To Use:

- 2 eggs
- 1 tub of whipped cream
- 10 crushed peanut butter cookies
- ¾ cup of granulated sugar
- 2 cups of water
- 10 cups for chocolate peanuts butter
- 2 packages of cream cheese
- 1/3 cup of creamy peanut butter
- 3 cups of unsalted butter

Step-by-Step Directions to Cook It:

1. Mix melted butter with crushed peanut butter cookies
2. Pour the mixture inside the air fry pan
3. Use a mixer to mix eggs, cream cheese, peanut butter, and sugar
4. Put the peanut butter cups on the crust in the pan
5. Pour the egg mixture into the cups
6. Put the pan in the Ninja Foodi XL Pro Air Fry Oven
7. Start the oven and press the bake mode for 25 minutes at 3600F
8. Allow cooling before serving

Serving Suggestion: serve with whipped cream

Preparation and Cooking Tips: set the oven at the précised mode

Nutritional value per serving: Calories: 640kcal, Fat: 48g, Carb: 50g, Proteins: 15g

Jelly Puffs with Chocolate Peanut Butter

This is a nutritious and yummy recipe. It is the perfect and healthy dessert for every moment

Preparation time: 25 minutes
Cooking time: 15 minutes
Serves: 5

Ingredients To Use:

- 16 tsp of creamy peanut butter
- 1 tbsp of whole milk
- 1 tube of flaky biscuit dough
- 1 cup of confectioners' sugar
- Chocolate milk bars
- ¼ cup of raspberry jam
- Cooking spray

Step-by-Step Directions to Cook It:

1. Peel the biscuit into half using the separation
2. Cut chocolates into 16 pieces
3. Drizzle baking pan with cooking spray
4. Open the biscuit, put 1 tsp of butter on the half biscuit, put a piece of chocolate on it
5. Put an edge on the dough on its chocolate, make a ball shape with it
6. Put the biscuit mix on the air fry pan, repeat for the remaining biscuit
7. Place the biscuit balls in the Ninja Foodi XL Pro Air Fry Oven
8. Start the oven and press the bake mode for 20 minutes at 3600F
9. Mix milk, jam, and confectioners' sugar in a bowl for the frosting
10. Serve biscuit with frosting top when it is cool

Serving Suggestion: serve with cream
Preparation and Cooking Tips: mix the puff according to the procedure
Nutritional value per serving: Calories: 660kcal, Fat: 26g, Carb: 50g, Proteins: 15g

Chocolate Crème

Chocolate crème is a sweet and flavourful recipe. It is very nutritious and easy to cook.
Preparation time: 15 minutes
Cooking time: 20 minutes
Serves: 4

Ingredients To Use:

- 1 tbsp of chocolate sprinkles
- 1 ½ cups of heavy cream
- Salt
- Whipped cream
- ½ cup of whole milk
- 5 big eggs
- ¼ cup of caster sugar
- ½ cup of whole milk

Step-by-Step Directions to Cook It:

1. Mix milk and heavy cream in a bowl
2. Mix salt, egg, and sugar in a bowl and whisk well
3. Add the 2 mixtures together and pour it into 4 ramekins
4. Put the ramekins in the Ninja Foodi XL Pro Air Fry Oven for 20 minutes at 3600F
5. Serve immediately

Serving Suggestion: serve with whipped cream and chocolate sprinkles

Preparation and Cooking Tips: mix the ingredients well

Nutritional value per serving: Calories: 395kcal, Fat: 27g, Carb: 33g, Proteins: 8g

Cheesecake in New York Style

This is a mouthwatering cheesecake. It is a good dessert after lunch.
Preparation time: 15 minutes
Cooking time: 50 minutes
Serves: 4

Ingredients To Use:

- 1 ½ Tbsp of brown sugar
- 12 graham crackers
- 1 cup of granulated sugar
- ½ cup of sour cream
- 1 tsp of vanilla extract
- 2 tbsp of melted butter
- 2 tbsp of arrowroot starch
- Salt
- 2 egg
- 16 ounces of cream cheese

Step-by-Step Directions to Cook It:

1. Crush the graham cracker
2. Pour the crushed crackers inside a bowl, add butter and brown sugar, and mix
3. Spoon the mixture inside the air fry pan, pour a cup of water in it
4. Put the pan in the Ninja Foodi XL Pro Air Fry Oven
5. Start the air fry and press the bake mode for 6 minutes at 350oF
6. Use the mixture to mix eggs, granulated sugar, vanilla, sour cream, salt, cream cheese, and arrowroot starch
7. Pour the mixture on the crust, bake for another 25 minutes
8. Allow cheesecake to cool down before serving

Serving Suggestion: serve with juice
Preparation and Cooking Tips: mix the ingredients homogenously
Nutritional value per serving: Calories: 740kcal, Fat: 54g, Carb: 42g, Proteins: 26g

Conclusion

Now that you know the value of the Ninja Foodi 10-in-1 XL Pro Air fry Toaster Oven, it is natural to be eager to start applying all the recipes in this cookbook to make your best meals ever.

Good Luck!